How Do You Spank a Porcupine?

* * * * *

BY **RONALD ROOD**

The New England Press
Shelburne, Vermont

ISBN 0-933050-19-4
Library of Congress Catalog Card Number: 83-62565

Originally published by Simon & Schuster, Inc.
(Former ISBN 671-27022-2)

For additional copies or for a catalog of our books,
please write:

The New England Press
P.O. Box 575
Shelburne, VT 05482

How
Do You Spank
a Porcupine?

Sweet are the uses of adversity;
Which, like the toad, ugly and venomous,
Wears yet a precious jewel in his head;
And this our life, exempt from public haunt,
Finds tongues in trees, books in the running brooks,
Sermons in stones, and good in every thing.

—As you Like It, *Act II, Scene 1*

1

WHEN WE PLANNED the picnic, we figured it would be a pretty quiet affair. Our church picnics usually were, except for the time when somebody left the chicken pie out in the sun too long. This unfortunate lapse gave almost everybody a case of dyspepsia and forced us to call the softball game in the third inning. And, of course, there was the occasion on which the minister delivered a little sermon entitled "Do as I say, not as I do"—and then promptly ran off with the choir director.

But since I was now the choir director and my wife was right there in the alto section, there seemed to be no reason why this should not be an ordinary picnic. Certainly there was no reason to suspect that I'd start out on an afternoon stroll with the women's chorus and come back stripped to the waist.

Actually, given my interest in the world of nature, I suppose I should always be prepared for the unexpected. Ever since childhood I've been intrigued with anything that swims, crawls, flies, or just plain stands there. Just as some people will swerve their car to avoid a cat or dog in the road, I'll dodge around a mixed-up beetle or one of those black-and-brown woolly caterpillars. I suppose my erratic course is a bit unnerving to other motorists, but my wife Peg says it helps keep her awake.

Our property in Vermont is ideal for a nature lover. About a hundred acres of meadows and hilly woods with a river along its edge, it encourages all kinds of wildlife. A few years ago we laid out a nature trail through the woods. At intervals, we thoughtfully placed labels that told what kind of a bramble it was that had just raveled your sweater, or what kind of twig you'd just collected in your eye.

But if you endured the trail you emerged on a little pond at the upper edge of our land, which, we told ourselves, was worth it all. It was along this trail, on that last Thursday in May, that I walked with the women's chorus—all unsuspecting.

Rebel, of course, was with us. Half beagle, half fox terrier, our little dog goes along on all our walks. When he stumbles across a rabbit in the woods, he announces the fact with a series of joyous yelps. Then his voice rises and falls as the rabbit leads him through the forest. Finally his bounding quarry tires of the game and pops into a hole. Then Rebel comes panting back to us, with a look that seems to say, "I'd have caught him sure if he'd only played fair."

This afternoon, just as we came to the point where a little brook crosses the trail, Rebel burst into full voice up ahead.

One of the women in the group listened for a moment. "Rabbit?" she asked.

I nodded. "Now you'll hear him take off through the woods."

We resumed our walk. But the sound of Reb's barking didn't change direction; it remained in one place—eager and louder as we approached. If rabbits could climb, I'd have sworn he had it treed.

Now we were separated from the dog by no more than twenty paces. I could see the white curl of Rebel's tail waving through a break in the undergrowth like a flag in the heat of battle. Putting a finger to my lips, I tiptoed ahead. Behind me, single file, came the chorus, all seven of them.

Rebel looked up as we came into view. Encouraged by the sight of eight human beings, he doubled his efforts. Jumping forward, he gave a loud bark—then tumbled backward with a startled yelp.

I looked at him in amazement. That white banner was tucked between his legs. The black fur stood up in a ridge along his back and over his shoulders.

I'd seen him look like this before, but what caught my eye was the appearance of his nose and mouth. He'd suddenly grown a new set of whiskers.

But in the next moment, I realized that these weren't his whiskers at all. That stubble on his chin hadn't been there when he'd started on our little walk. He had acquired it in the last ten seconds. And, although I still couldn't see the creature that was causing all the fuss, I knew what we'd find—a porcupine. Rebel had run up against it in his last dash, and the quill-pig had left him with a snootful of stiff, barbed quills.

I bent over the unhappy dog. When I reached to pull out one of the quills, he saw my hand coming and jerked away. Trying again, I got the same result, but this time he snapped at my fingers. Of course he was immediately apologetic for such unseemly action. But he was miserable, and his misery wanted no company.

Releasing our deflated pet for a moment, I turned to look for the porcupine. He was not going to make a dartboard out of *my* dog. . . .

But somehow his opponent had escaped. All I could see were a few leaves and a clod of earth. There was no sign of the animal. The arena was deserted.

"Must be a hole in the ground," I remarked, as I stepped closer. "That porcupine didn't just evaporate."

"Look out!" Bessie Pixley warned with a sharp intake of breath. "You'll get quilled!"

"Nonsense," I said. "I won't get quilled until I see him."

"He's right there, Ron. One step ahead of you."

I was about to remark on Bessie's eyesight when I detected a small movement on the forest floor. Now I realized that what I'd assumed to be leaves and a loose piece of soil was the arching back and defiant quills of a porcupine.

And what a porcupine! It was scarcely larger than my clenched fist—the tiniest one of its kind I had ever seen. Keeping its back turned to me it presented an array of short black-and-white quills in a regular sunburst pattern.

A whimper from behind told me that Rebel was taking it all in. "Why, Rebel," I said in amazement, "did all those quills come from that little . . ."

I never finished the sentence because just at that moment the porcupine flipped its spiny tail. Several leaves had apparently fallen across his tail as Rebel fled; now the leaves sprayed into the air with the force of the thrust. At the sound of the sharp movement, all of us, including the dog, jumped.

Recovering my poise, I tried to uphold my position as leader of the group. "Kinda startled you, didn't it?" I said patronizingly. "But don't worry—he can't throw his quills."

Now the ladies found their voices.

"I thought they spent their time in the trees," one said. "What's he doing here?"

"Maybe he fell down," another volunteered. With that, we all looked up dutifully into the arching canopy of leaves but it revealed nothing.

The next thought was that he'd lost his mother. Ordinarily, the ladies wouldn't have gone looking for a bereft porcupine, but this tiny creature had aroused their maternal instincts. I warned them, however, that the mother would be just as defensive as her baby, and that they should pursue the search for her with great care.

Soon it was obvious that the silent little being who stood his ground there in the middle of nowhere was the only porcupine in the area. We knew now that we had an orphan on our hands.

And a miserable pup. Rebel was shaking his head and trying to wipe his muzzle with his paw without actually touching it. I squatted down and looked at him again. He bristled with perhaps three dozen quills.

They weren't very long, having come from such a tiny creature. The largest was perhaps only half an inch in length. But it's a good idea to remove a porky's quills as quickly as possible, even if they're just tiny ones, because the barbs are shaped in such a way that they penetrate the flesh more deeply with each motion of the victim. We decided to operate there in the woods, whether Rebel liked it or not.

Transfixing the luckless pet with a no-nonsense stare, we advanced. He tried to slink away but I managed to catch him and while Peg held his head and the United Church choir held his body, I set to work. Fortunately, Rebel hadn't actually tried to bite the little quill-pig, so there were no spines inside his mouth. But I winced as much as he did when we tweaked the quills out of his lips, nose, and moustache-area. I found that I could pull most of them out with my fingers. Two or three, however, would have to wait until we got home where we could use a pair of pliers. The ordeal took perhaps ten minutes. When we were finished there were several tiny drops of blood where the barbs had stuck.

At that, he was lucky. Porcupines are common creatures in the north woods, and many dogs have had painful encounters with them. I recall hearing about one dog who ran afoul of a full-grown porky. Helpless with distress, she made her way under the porch of a house. No amount of coaxing would bring her out, and the porch floor finally had to be torn up to get her. There were patches on her face that were solid with quills, some more than four inches long and almost as large around as a soda straw. Her mouth was so full of spines that she couldn't close it.

Her owners managed to bundle her into the car and take her to the veterinarian who gave her a knockout shot and extracted more than two hundred quills—any one of which could have been fatal had it worked its way into her brain.

I returned now to the porcupine that had caused it all. For most of our neighbors the sight of a porcupine means one thing: get rid of it, and fast. Porkies chew the bark of trees, sometimes girdling them, and they attack twigs and buds. They are also attracted to anything with salt on it; objects such as a sweaty ax-handle or the wood of a cabin door can be completely destroyed by their gnawing teeth. And, as Reb discovered, they can cause inquisitive animals great distress.

For these reasons porcupines are greeted with something less than joy. But ours wasn't just any porcupine. It was an orphan, alone in the forest. You don't turn your back on an orphan. Not even if its back is turned on you.

We stood and contemplated the scene. "Well?" somebody said, "what do we do now?"

"Aren't you going to take him home and feed him?" somebody else asked.

"Sure," I said. "Carry him home in my bare hands, I suppose."

My own words gave me a thought. I glanced at the members of the group. It had been a warm evening but I noticed that Gyneth Hartwell had a nice fluffy sweater. Somehow she sensed my question before I even asked it.

"Oh, no, you don't," she said. "Nobody's going to wrap a porcupine in my sweater. All those quills? Never."

Hopefully I looked at the other ladies. But none of them had a piece of clothing to offer the little one-pound waif.

That left only me.

"—but this is my best sport shirt," I protested. "Sent to me by my brother . . ."

Silence.

". . . all the way from Hawaii," I concluded, as I undid the fancy wooden buttons.

Then, like a bullfighter with his cape, I held my shirt before me and advanced on that black ball of stickers.

Gingerly I wrapped him in the shirt, holding the cloth with my fingertips. He tried to lash out with his tail, but the folds of the cloth confined his movements. Finally I scooped him up.

He was astonishingly light. Having handled baby rabbits, squirrels, woodchucks, and even skunks, I had guessed that he would weigh more. But it was almost as if I had picked up a handful of leaves. So now we knew for sure: he *was* an orphan, and a half-starved one at that.

Taking turns holding the silent little creature at arm's length, we retraced our steps to the house. By the time we arrived darkness had fallen.

I thought of how lonesome it must have been on

previous nights for a motherless porcupine. Turning on the kitchen light, we managed to relieve Rebel of the few quills he had left. Then we set the porcupine in the middle of the floor and tried to remove the shirt.

It wasn't easy. His protesting body had remained staunchly at attention all the way home. Now he was practically bonded to the cloth. I could see the black quills whose invisible, backward-pointing barbs prevented us from pulling away the shirt.

But I knew he had to be relieved of his straitjacket somehow so, starting at one end, I began to work away the cloth, little by little.

My efforts were finally successful, but in the process the animal parted with scores of his stickers. The smallest were coal black and about a quarter-inch in length. Others, three times as long, were white with black tips.

The porcupine was so tightly huddled that his entire surface presented one continuous mass of stiff hairs and spines. The loss of a hundred stickers, more or less, apparently hadn't thinned his defenses a bit.

Buried down in that living cactus, there were two eyes, two ears, and a nose. But the only way we could identify the head was the manner in which he turned as one of us approached him. As we changed position, so did he—placing himself so that his murderous little tail would be the first thing we'd encounter if we dared reach for him.

To test him, I brushed him with the shirt. At that slight touch, the tail snapped up, leaving several more souvenirs in the cloth.

As we were pondering our next move, the children, Alison and Roger, came home from a high school softball game. Curious about a porcupine's eating habits, they decided to look through some of the books on my shelves.

"Porcupines begin to nibble on buds and shoots within a day or two after birth," announced Alison, reading aloud from one volume.

Roger's book wasn't quite so positive. "Porcupines are said to be able to take care of themselves at an early age. Their food is similar to that of the parents."

A third book hedged even further. "After birth," it stated helpfully, "the single young follows the mother about until it is able to make its own way in the forest."

I could see that we were going to have some difficulty finding the proper food for our prickle-pig. But, since the choir had to practice, I sent my children back upstairs for more information while we gathered around the piano. We left the porcupine huddled silently in the middle of the kitchen floor.

With most of our thoughts centered on what might be taking place in the other room, we cut our rehearsal short. Then, tiptoeing softly, we returned to the kitchen. Motioning everyone for silence, I carefully opened the door. I wanted to see what a porcupine would be doing without an audience.

We needn't have hurried. And we needn't have worried. The porcupine hadn't moved. Except for a slight relaxing of those quills—which he brought back to full mast the instant he was aware of our presence—he was just as we'd left him. And there he remained, a little ball of hostility.

"Well?" somebody asked for the second time that evening. "What do we do now?"

Peg and I have had a fair share of experience with animals. She was my assistant in the zoology laboratory at college when I was a lofty senior and she was but a sophomore. And, shortly after graduation when I realized what a fine help she'd been, and how expensive she would be to replace, I married her. She's been my helper for twenty-six years now—though neither of us has figured out the economics of the business. With all that experience behind us, we should have known what to do.

But this was not a helpless little fox cub, searching blindly for the warm dugs of his mother. It wasn't a spotted fawn that sucked trustingly at a proffered finger. Nor was it a newly hatched grouse, so eager to fill its little crop that we had only to toss an insect in its general direction. This was a tiny orphan porcupine, bent on self-protection—yet all alone against the world and starving.

"What do we do now?" I pondered aloud. "Take care of him. Give him a place to sleep. Feed him."

"How are you going to feed him?"

"I don't know, exactly. Probably with a medicine dropper."

This idea tickled everybody. It was an intriguing thought: tucking a dropper into that resistant ball of pins, hoping to hit his mouth—and pretending it was Momma.

Come to think of it, I hadn't even *seen* his mouth yet. Nor, for that matter, his nose, his eyes, or his ears. In fact, I wasn't sure I'd even seen his head, although I knew it was probably tucked down near his front feet.

We decided not to try to feed him that evening. He'd had quite a day, and I suspected from the strength he'd shown, he'd at least survive the night. In the morning, after he'd had a chance to get used to his new surroundings, he might not be quite so negative.

Peg found a large pasteboard carton and made a bed out of old rags and newspaper. Then, placing the carton on its side, we pushed the porcupine into it, bulldozer fashion. Carefully righting the carton, we slid it into the corner of the kitchen. Peg dropped in a few lettuce leaves and I added a garnish of hemlock from one of the trees in our yard. I figured that in case he got the urge to eat during the night, he'd have something with which he could experiment.

The ladies of the choir gathered up the dishes they'd brought to the picnic and prepared to leave. Solemnly filing past the box on their way out, they looked as if they were paying their last respects at a funeral.

"Well," said Peg, as their cars vanished into the Vermont night, "that's that, dear. All but your porcupine."

I corrected her. "All but *our* porcupine. After all, you found him, too. In fact, it's Rebel's porcupine. If it hadn't been for Rebel, nobody would have found him."

We contemplated our beagle–fox terrier. He was maintaining a respectful distance from the porcupine. Asleep on the floor, he yipped and twitched his legs as if he were back on the trail.

"Anyway," countered Peg, " 'sufficient unto the day,' or something. You'll probably be up half the night worrying about him. Why not turn in now and get a little sleep first?"

So we shut Rebel out of the kitchen as a safety precaution. Then we retired for the night, leaving the porcupine in his cardboard box to fight his little battle alone.

2

PEG WAS RIGHT, of course. I couldn't just go to sleep and forget the porcupine. Twice during the night I stole downstairs for a look at him. The second time I found Alison sitting in a chair beside his box.

"He's awful quiet, Dad. Do you think he'll be all right?"

I glanced down at that silent prisoner in his pasteboard cell. Alison would gladly have traded places with him if she could. Always generous and kindhearted toward any creature, she couldn't bear to see an animal suffer needlessly. During her earlier years, when she found a dead bird or mouse by the road, she'd bring it home and give it a burial with full honors in the cool soil of our yard. Now, at seventeen, she has learned to accept such roadside casualties. But this was no casualty. Not yet, anyway. It was a live porcupine.

"Oh, he'll be fine, Alison," I said in my most encouraging voice. "Tell you what—why don't we both go back to sleep? Maybe he'll be ready to make friends in the morning."

So we went upstairs. But in the morning he was as stubborn as ever. Most of the books had said porcupines ate green shoots and young leaves, so I took Roger up into the woods. There we gathered spring beauties, dwarf ginseng, dogtooth violets, hepatica leaves, wood anemones, tender ferns, and a few sprouted beech nuts. To these we added hemlock, woodsy-smelling balsam fir, and maple sugar for flavor.

"That ought to fix him," I said as I topped the salad off with a brown mushroom from the base of a decaying stump. "There's got to be something in this mess that he likes. We've got half the forest here."

Carefully we lowered the materials down to the porcupine. He flipped that muscular tail a couple of times, but gave no other sign. Hopefully, however, we carried his box out onto the front porch where he wouldn't be disturbed.

"Of course," Peg said, "there's one food he doesn't have in all this conglomeration. And I bet it's just the one he needs."

I'd had it in mind, too, ever since we brought him into the house. It was the universal food of baby animals. "Milk?" I asked, somewhat unnecessarily. She nodded. "With a medicine dropper."

I thought of the cooperation we'd get from that rigid little ball of stickers. "And who," I asked, "is going to hold the medicine dropper?"

"Oh, that's easy," she said. "I am, of course. You can hold the porcupine."

I cogitated on this for a while. We had force-fed enough protesting wild animals to know it'd be a job. It's bad enough to try to get a little milk into any recalcitrant youngster without having him back up his opinions with a handful of prickers.

Since Peg had to go to teach her kindergarten class shortly, we decided to leave the porcupine alone with his greenery until school let out in the afternoon. I was writing an article for a magazine, but several times during the day I paused to look in on him. Throughout the morning he occupied the same spot, but by the time the children came home from school he had moved to another corner of the box.

Well, now. Here was progress. It was the most activity he'd shown since we had gotten him. His pioneering spirit hadn't extended to the food, however. So, when Peg drove into the yard, I knew the time had arrived.

I set about mixing the formula. In the process of keeping alive the offspring of everything from deer mice to deer, we've hit upon a mixture which seems to work well. Consisting of a tablespoon of honey, a scant eighth-teaspoon of salt, and a cup of warm milk, it is quite palatable, even to humans. It has just enough sweetness to be interesting and enough salt to appeal to the animal's normal craving for this mineral.

It has another advantage, too. The honey makes it a bit sticky. So, even if the young animal balks at feeding, we just smear it on his lips. Later, he discovers from licking his lips that it's good—and soon he takes it eagerly.

Medicine droppers are fine for little rabbits, kittens, and—we hoped—porcupines. Baby bottles serve for larger animals while cotton swabs hold enough milk to start tiny mice and chipmunks. For those delicate creatures, cotton seems preferable to the hard glass of a medicine dropper.

Formula ready, we donned our porcupine-feeding uniforms. Peg had a light pair of leather gloves and a poplin jacket. After all, the most ferocious thing she expected to handle was the medicine dropper. My outfit was made of sturdier stuff. Roger's heavy ski gloves would fit over my hands. These plus my leather jacket, I hoped, would be adequate for the job. I had handled porcupines before, and had a deep respect for the penetrating power of those quills— even little ones.

Alison watched us gird for battle. Then she came up with a suggestion. "Let me just try first with the medicine dropper," our daughter pleaded. "Maybe if I speak to him real nice, he'll know we're his friends."

I offered her my heavy gloves, but she scorned them. She said just the sight of them would scare him to death. "Just Mother's gloves will be enough," she stated, as Peg handed them over to her.

We were both glad to let her have the first try. In order to allow her to get down on the porcupine's own level, we cut the box at the corners. Pressing the sides down flat, Alison lay on her stomach. Medicine dropper in one hand, saucepan of warm milk in the other, she inched toward him.

"Nice 'pine," she crooned, presenting the dropper. "Here's your milk."

In a flash the dropper flew out of her hand. Quick as thought, the little stranger had whirled and slapped at the offending object with his tail.

Undaunted, she hunched around until she was able to approach from another direction. "Here, 'pine," she said. But again he whirled and slapped.

After two or three more attempts she looked up at us in despair. "How can I even *try* to feed him," she asked, "when all he does is face me backwards?"

So there was nothing to do but to force him to eat. Donning our leather armor, we advanced to the task. Squatting down, I spoke in what I hoped was a reassuring tone. Then, reaching forward, I closed my leather gloves around his taut little body.

Grasping him with both hands, I lifted him and

turned him over. For the first time we saw the underside of our porcupine.

He held his black feet tightly together. The front ones were like little hands with four fingers and no thumb. The rear ones were like human feet. Long curved claws, perfect for his life in the trees, were held in front of his face. His square nose was tucked behind his front feet, and his eyes were tightly shut. We could only guess at the location of his rounded ears under the protective coat of fur and spines.

His head was hidden so far down between his feet that I had to hold him on his back. Then, while the four of us held our breaths, my wife poked the medicine dropper down between those curved black claws.

There was no question when the dropper found its mark. Up to now, the porcupine had not made a sound beyond the slight rustle of his quills, or the click of his toenails on the kitchen floor. But the combination of being restrained and attacked by the medicine dropper at the same time was too much. With a squeal he burst into action. Striking outward with those claws and biting fiercely at the medicine dropper, he tried to rid himself of all his tormentors at once. Between bites, his teeth chattered steadily, like a toy machine gun.

Peg, however, held her ground. And I held the porcupine. After he quieted down, she tried once more. Again came the battle. Luckily, the roundness of the medicine dropper prevented him from getting a good grip, or he'd have surely bitten it in half. I knew this when he turned and sank those orange teeth into the thumb of my heavy glove. But I just pulled my thumb back inside the glove, and let him chew on the leather while Peg waited.

When he finally calmed down, she presented the dropper a third time. He fought again, but not quite as viciously. As we all paused for rest, we noted the first sign of a breakthrough: though his eyes were still closed, a small pink tongue appeared in the darkness of his face. It licked his lips, and vanished as suddenly as it had come.

Quickly Peg smeared some more food on his lips. Again the tongue. But when she tried to give him the medicine dropper directly, he fought as before. Alison and Roger tried as well, but he wouldn't have anything to do with that dropper. So all three of them took turns daubing until his underside—and my ski gloves—were a mess.

At last, when my hands ached from holding his squirming body, we decided to call it quits. Milk dripping from both my elbows, I put the sticky creature in a new box. Then, as I extracted quills from the ski gloves, we tried to decide how much milk he'd probably consumed.

We'd used about a half-cup of the mixture, we figured, but much of it was still on his belly, chin, and legs. If he licked himself clean, he'd end up with perhaps a tablespoon. Not bad; his stomach probably didn't hold much more than that at one time, anyway.

Like most baby animals, he'd have to be fed a little bit at a sitting—if you could call it a sitting—and he'd have to be fed often.

At least there was hope. It might take half our waking hours to get enough milk into him, but it could be done. And as soon as he realized that the milk came from the dropper, it should be simple.

We tried again after supper, and again before retiring. More fight, more smear, more mess. He wasn't giving an inch. And in between times he remained as intractable as ever.

The second morning, after another stormy session, I put him back in his box. "Porcupine," I told him as I rinsed my sticky gloves and sleeves and prepared to pull out the current crop of quills, "for two cents, I'd haul you back to the woods and let you starve."

Alison, of course, knew I was only fooling. But even the thought of such a possibility disturbed her. So she set about to make the porcupine her special concern. Enlisting Roger's help, she replaced the wilted greenery we'd provided, even though it hadn't been disturbed. She added some lettuce, clover, catnip, and grass, and in her own gentle way, a homemade oatmeal cookie.

She stepped back and looked at her small charge.

He was almost bedded down in food. "I know what he needs," she decided. "He needs a mother."

At this Roger laughed. "Like you, for instance?"

Alison sniffed. "It's not funny. How'd *you* like to be all alone in a box on somebody's porch without your own warm—"

She stopped in midsentence, her eyes wide. Then, without a word, she ran for the stairs.

Going quickly to her room, she rummaged around in her closet. I heard her asking Peg where we kept the heating pad. Soon she returned with the pad and her old teddy bear.

"Now," she said to anybody who was listening, "you watch."

She slipped the pad under the corner of the box where the porcupine was huddled, and placed the teddy bear near him. Then she trimmed a small cardboard carton, cutting out one side so it could be inverted over the porcupine and provide an exit if he desired. Carefully, she lowered his domicile in place.

"There," she announced, as she snapped on the heating pad. "I bet we're getting somewhere."

I had to admit that it made sense. Our various orphan birds and animals had always been supplied with a nest of rags or soft grass, though we'd never gone so far as to provide a stuffed toy for a companion. And the heating pad was perfectly logical, too. Nobody had thought of it before, since the weather had been warm. But a small porcupine, bedding down with his mother in a hollow stump or rocky cave, would sense the warmth of her body. The cardboard carton, of course, provided the "cave."

Now the question was to find out if the friendly atmosphere did anything to alter his attitude toward life. Alison wouldn't let anybody disturb him for the rest of the morning. "He's got to get used to it," she explained.

At noon we warmed up his milk and donned our feeding outfits. Then the four of us knelt around his box. We peered down like surgeons over an operating table while Alison carefully lifted the walls and ceiling of the little porcupine's room.

The sight of our porcupine must have surprised even Alison. Lying on his stomach alongside the teddy bear, he was sound asleep. Both rear legs were stretched out behind him and we could see the black soles of his flat feet. His chin rested between his forepaws. And, for the first time, we saw how he looked without his quills raised. The long guard hairs covered the quills almost completely, and their darkness made him appear almost jet black.

Not daring to make a sound, Alison looked at me questioningly. Should we let the porcupine sleep, or wake him up and feed him?

As we silently pondered our next move Roger pointed to a shred of greenery, and nodded vehemently. It was all that was left of the piece of lettuce we'd put in earlier.

Smiling happily, Alison basked in the glory of victory. Then she gingerly replaced the box. Tiptoeing backward, we retreated to the kitchen to congratulate her. The woman's touch had made the difference. Our baby porcupine might survive after all.

He slept most of the afternoon. But when we tried to feed him later, we again encountered resistance.

There was no doubt about the success of the teddy bear, however. No matter where we put it in his box, he'd press as close to it as his coat of quills would allow. Even when they were relaxed, those quills, standing out on all sides, reminded me of a little girl's crinoline dress.

At feeding time, he continued to be unyielding. Occasionally, he'd eat some of the lettuce we gave him, and he finally condescended to put a few toothmarks in Alison's cookie. But he wouldn't budge as far as the medicine dropper was concerned. Every feeding was an ordeal—for all of us.

Then, one evening, he collapsed.

That's the only way I can describe it. For some reason apparent only to him, he suddenly decided to cooperate, just like that.

It was about a week after we'd found him. Alison was holding him with those heavy gloves and Peg was aiming one medicine dropperful of milk after another in the general direction of his protesting mouth. Watching with those little black eyes, he'd anticipate each new offering and do his best to bat it away with his feet or bite it with his teeth.

My wife and daughter were talking to him as they struggled. I was reading in the other room, glancing up now and then, but actually paying little attention to their efforts. Then I realized that Peg was talking to me.

"Ron," she said, in the same even tone of voice they'd been using for the past few minutes, "come carefully. Look at your porcupine now."

I didn't have to look. My ears told me all I needed to know. There was a new sound in the kitchen—a sound familiar to any parent who has ever given a bottle to a baby. Of course it was pitched two octaves higher, because of the porcupine's tiny vocal cords, but it was unmistakable—the rhythmic noise a baby makes as it sucks contentedly on the bottle. Our porcupine was taking his milk right from the dropper.

Now he seemed to be insatiable. Peg dipped the dropper and presented it in an almost continual motion. Whereas before, each dropperful had been a matter of waiting for just the right moment and then smearing it quickly in the general vicinity of his mouth, it now lasted for just about four good swallows.

Finally he'd had enough. "Thank goodness," sighed Peg, as she laid the medicine dropper aside at last, "that's over."

Alison held him up so we could inspect him. We could see the soft, unprotected underside—the large chink in the porcupine's armor. While his bleary little eyes surveyed us from his lofty height, he finished the remnants of his meal with that startlingly pink tongue. Then, before I could protest, Alison gently lowered him to her shoulder. "Watch this," her eyes said.

We stood motionless with surprise. One flip of that tail, one impulsive jerk of that body could drive a dozen barbed spikes deep into the flesh of her neck and cheek. But somehow, she knew it wouldn't happen. With a little smile on her face, she remained perfectly still while the porcupine investigated her.

He stood for a moment and contemplated the unknown world beyond the angle of her shoulder. Sniffing and blinking, he stretched out as far as he could. Then, feeling backward with his tail, he lowered himself a few inches down her sleeve and blouse. The close-woven fabric didn't supply much of a toehold, however, so he regained his position. Now there remained but one other place to investigate. Inching forward, he sniffed at her collar, then at her neck.

Alison held her breath. The porcupine raised himself on his haunches and nuzzled in her hair. Then my daughter squinted her eyes tight. "He tickles!" she blurted.

The porcupine had poked around until he found her ear. Now he gently nipped it, at the same time uttering an entirely new sound—a series of high-pitched little grunts: hunh-hunh-hunh.

Alison caught her breath even as she tried to talk. She clenched her fists, hunched her back, and grimaced as if someone had turned on a cold shower. Finally she managed to get out a few words.

"S-see?" she gasped. "I probably . . . smell the same . . . to him . . . as my teddy bear. I told you . . . all he wanted was a . . . m-mother. That's all."

3

ONCE HIS FORTRESS had fallen, our small guest was a different creature. He did an about-face—literally and figuratively. Instead of being quills, back, and tail, he now was sniffing nose, shoe-button eyes, and beseeching black paws.

His box became too small for him the instant he acquired his new personality. He wasn't content with merely crouching in the corner. He stood on his hind legs and reached as high as he could. Propped by his muscular tail, he shuffled around the inside of the box, looking up and feeling for the top edge that was just beyond his grasp.

Peg and I watched him after Alison had returned him to his cardboard home. "He's got to have something better than that," I decided. "After all, out in the wild he'd probably spend most of his time up in a tree."

"Well, then," said Peg, "let's get him a tree."

She was probably joking, but there was something in the suggestion. "That's an idea," I agreed. "We'll find him a good climbing tree."

My wife looked at me in surprise. "You must be kidding. How long do you think he'd stay in it? He'd probably wander away during the night and starve to death."

"No, no, Peg. I mean cut a tree and bring it to him."

She looked at me. "And where, may I ask, do we have room for a tree?"

I thought for a moment. "How about the front porch?"

"Whose front porch did you have in mind?"

We were at it again. It's sort of a running battle between us. Peg loves the outdoors and its creatures as much as I do. She balks, however, when I suggest that we give a portion of our living quarters to the latest waif in need of a home. Love me, love my dog, I figure, but she doesn't always see it that way. As a result, it's been an uphill struggle for both of us over these twenty-six years.

I had seen no reason, for instance, not to keep a jarful of black widow spiders on my windowsill. After all, I was writing an article on this shy creature at the time. But Peg couldn't seem to see it. Finally, she capitulated and said I could keep them—on the outside, with the window shut.

It was the same way with the frogs in the refrigerator and the woodchuck in the cellar. Reasonable enough, I thought. After all, frogs spend the winter sleeping in the frozen mud, so I wouldn't have to feed them if I kept them cold. The woodchuck had been boosted out of hibernation by a bulldozer so I figured he'd just dig into the dirt walls of our old farmhouse cellar and go back to sleep again.

Peg, of course, recalled these events as we talked about foresting the front porch. But I pointed out that our past efforts had turned out just fine. It had been a real experience during one winter to open the icebox and be greeted by the sight of a bunch of frogs in their cozy jug. And then, in March, when I released them into the new beaver-pond, they had laid a batch of eggs to start their own version of a population explosion.

The woodchuck had made his own exit in due time by tunneling his way through the cellar wall. The hole in the lawn where he finally emerged was merely an added bonus. I discovered it when I smacked into it with the lawnmower.

With these reminders of past successes, Peg finally agreed to having the porcupine on the porch, "to see what can possibly happen next," as she put it. So Alison and I went up along the little brook which flows down into our pasture from the woods. I had seen evidence of porcupine chewings in the trees there last winter. Perhaps if we could find them again we'd know what kind of tree porkies preferred, although I knew they usually weren't fussy.

Finally we found a little yellow birch. Standing about fifteen feet high, it had been stripped to the bare wood on one side. I could hardly blame the porky; yellow birch bark has a delightful wintergreen smell. Commercial wintergreen extract is often made from twigs of this tree as well as from those of the related black birch. So I cut down the tree, dragged it back to the house, trimmed it, and set it in a pan of water in a corner of the porch. Then we covered the pan with a few evergreen boughs so the porcupine wouldn't get a dunking as he climbed around.

We carried our small friend, box and all, out to his new quarters. "There," said Alison as she picked him up and put him halfway up the tree, "now you're back in your forest."

The new playpen was an immediate success. Those curved black claws and stout little legs were unsure of themselves, but slowly they took him all over the limbs and trunk. He sniffed at the bark and nipped once or twice with those orange rodent teeth, but only succeeded in making a few scratches.

Like most beginners, he was cautious and a little wobbly. I've watched baby squirrels, chipmunks, and raccoons as they made their first venture in a tree. They cling so tightly and move so gingerly that they remind me of the comedians stranded on a skyscraper in the old movies.

Our porcupine was little better. His hind legs would grasp a limb tightly from both sides while he tentatively stretched ahead with an arm. Only after he tested his grip several times would he follow up with the other arm. And only when his front end was secure would he hitch his nether portion forward. Peg said he reminded her of a portly measuring worm.

After we'd watched him awhile, Alison put a few birch twigs in his box along with some fresh grass. And, of course, that teddy bear. "Now," she said as we went back into the house, "enjoy your new home, Little Pine."

And so Little Pine got his name and his living quarters. Soon we shortened his name just to Pine, and finally settled on Piney.

There. One hurdle was over. But the next one was just ahead. My son lost no time in pointing it out to me.

"We're going to keep him now, aren't we, Dad?"

"Sure, Roger. For a while."

"How long is a while?"

"Well, until he learns to take care of himself, I guess."

"What if he never learns?"

I reminded him of the system under which we'd been operating for years. My interests as a naturalist brought me into contact with all kinds of animals. People thought of me whenever they came across an orphaned bird, a wounded frog, or—on one impressive occasion—a skunk with its head caught in a tin can. As a result, we were constantly struggling between compassion and common sense. We had to be careful or our Vermont farm would have been turned into a zoo.

Thus we had set up our own code. We allowed an animal to stay around the house as long as it wished, but always kept in mind that it was a wild creature. When it wanted to go back to the wild again, we let it go.

Very few plots of ground are as pleasant for a convalescing animal as our hundred acres in Vermont. With a river forming the entire eastern boundary of the property, we're quite effectively insulated from the road beyond. In fact, our only physical contact with the outer world is a bridge which crosses to the road. Deep woods surround us in every other direction.

And should some wandering animal manage to negotiate the bridge, he would find the land on the other side of the road similar to ours—overgrown pasture, woods, and meadows. So a rehabilitated hawk trying a mended wing, or a reconditioned raccoon puddling along the river's edge need have little fear from man. There just aren't that many people around.

Should some curious creature wander even farther afield, to follow the river valley and its paralleling road, it would pass only two human habitations in the first mile in either direction. Farther upstream, it would come to the quiet woods of the Green Mountain National Forest. And, downstream, it would have to travel nearly two miles before it came to anything resembling a town—a handful of houses, the tiny bobbin mill, Brown's general store, and, of course, the inevitable little white church.

If the animal wandered in any other direction, it would soon be absorbed in the woods, ledges, and steep hillsides of our own land. Thus, we reason, a creature going out on its own has plenty of time to regain its wariness in the presence of man.

So I answered Roger's question by saying there was little chance that Piney would forget all his own wild ways. We'd keep him on the porch only as long as he needed milk and warmth and a sheltered place to sleep. When he outgrew such things, we'd prop the porch door open. Then, in his own good time, he'd make his way to the forest.

But there were complications. Piney was hopelessly attached to his teddy bear. When Alison put the fuzzy toy up in his tree, he'd snuggle up to it as soon as he wanted to go to sleep. If it fell to the floor, he'd make his way down to it again.

His general appearance was a bit unsettling, too. With his arms and legs able to bend startlingly like those of a human and his heavy coat of quills and fur rounding him out, Peg decided he looked like a little man in a snowsuit. Of course, once she'd said it, the idea stuck. Anytime he stood on his hind legs and propped himself up with that tail, there was our little person, about ten inches high.

There was one other problem and it didn't take us long to discover it. The porcupine was hopelessly nearsighted.

We had had animals before that weren't visually gifted. The raccoons we'd housed were able to spot movements a hundred feet away, but I was convinced they could see clearly for only half that distance. Two orphaned muskrats were scarcely any better. Although it's almost impossible to sneak up on a muskrat in the wild, it seems to be as much a matter of scent and hearing as it is of keen vision. Our two animals apparently had difficulty seeing clearly beyond twenty feet.

But they were eagle-eyed compared to Piney. We found this out during his first day in the tree. The four of us were standing nearby, watching as he climbed from one limb to another. None of us was more than five feet away. We observed him in silence for some time.

Finally Alison spoke. "He's a regular acrobat!"

Her words, though uttered in a normal tone, had an immediate effect. Instantly the porcupine bristled.

Then, recognizing Alison's voice, he slowly relaxed and sniffed in her general direction.

"Why, Piney," she said, "did I scare you?"

As she spoke, the porcupine raised up on his haunches. Moving his head from side to side, he zeroed in on her voice. Shifting a bit on his branch, he finally faced her squarely.

"He acts as if he hadn't even known we were here," Alison said in wonderment.

This gave me an idea. Holding a finger to my lips for silence, I slowly motioned to Alison to bend down.

The results were fantastic. My daughter carefully lowered herself until she was squatting right on the floor. And there she was: three feet below the porcupine while he continued to gaze steadfastly into space. He hadn't seen her at all.

Now she spoke to him again. "Here, Piney. Down here—see? Right below you."

It was so painfully evident—the porcupine could barely see beyond his nose.

We tested him further and finally decided that his visibility extended only about three feet, though he could detect motions at a greater distance.

As we contemplated this, I remembered a time my father and I had been fishing in a little rowboat. A fog had risen on the lake in a few minutes, enveloping us in a close-fitting shroud of vapor. There we had been forced to stay, becalmed, scarcely able to see each other at opposite ends of the boat. This, it occurred to me, is how it must feel to be a porcupine: you're on a tiny island of clarity, surrounded by an immense ocean of blur.

This, too, was going to complicate things when it came time to let him go. You could encourage a deer or a squirrel or a fox to make its way back to the wild. It would quickly learn to spot potential enemies at a distance. But by the time Piney fathomed the intentions—or even the identity—of some dimly seen object more than three or four feet away, it would be too late. A wild porcupine lives its entire life on the principle of defense, for it often travels with its quills half raised. But Piney had gone beyond that stage already. And he'd certainly be far past it by the time we could get him weaned.

Actually, we face a problem like this every time we give shelter to a wild creature. As the animal becomes more familiar with humans, its chances of success in returning safely to the woods diminish accordingly. It's almost certain death for a pet raccoon, say, or a squirrel, when a family decides they've had it long enough. When such a creature is "given its freedom," it has little knowledge of wild ways. It cannot even compete with its own kind.

We saw this starkly illustrated three summers ago. Linda Steadman, a friend of Alison's, had found a nest of bluejays in an old stump. The persistent clamoring of their voices told her something was wrong, so she kept an eye on the nest. When, during an entire afternoon, neither parent had returned, she decided the youngsters must have been deserted. So she improvised a nest for them in a shoebox and undertook to raise them herself.

They were hungry little youngsters. They gobbled bread soaked in milk almost as fast as she could feed it to them. But as they became more active, they nearly ran afoul of the neighbor's cat. So, reluctantly, she brought them to me.

"I just want you to let them go here at your place where no cat or dog is going to get them," Linda told me.

I looked at my new charges. They were beautiful birds. The incredible blue and immaculate white of their wings and tail contrasted with the black facial streaks and with the chocolate brown eyes which scrutinized my every move. The sturdy black beaks were full-sized, but still showed the little white edges at the corners which are the mark of the youngster in the bird kingdom. Plainly they were full-feathered and ready to fly.

"They'll follow you around everywhere," Linda said, as she held one on her finger and stroked its white breast. "I'd never part with them if there weren't so many cats around."

So I took Bluey and Snippy into our home. They were wonderfully engaging pets. Like all jays, they were thieving rascals, and snatched any bright object that caught their fancy. A piece of tinfoil or a white cigarette butt would be hidden in a corner of the front porch. They even found the charm bracelet Alison had lost a month before. And my shockproof watch got a sudden workout one day when Snippy squared off and gave it a whack.

But then, jays are like that. For eons they have lived a bold, brash existence. They have hammered out a living where lesser birds would fail. In fact, their livelihood is often at the expense of the eggs and young of their weaker neighbors. Jays are notorious nest-robbers. My mother used to say that their loud cry gave away their intentions: "Thief! Thief!"

Snippy and Bluey were personable creatures, however, and we forgave them their faults. You couldn't help but love the bluecoated little scamps.

They stayed close to the house, rarely venturing more than a few feet from the porch. But after we'd had them about a week, we had a picnic at the fireplace out in the front yard. Taking the jays out to the table with us, we tossed bits of hamburger out on the grass and watched them fly after them.

Suddenly there was a streak of greenish-blue through the air. Snippy ducked as a tree swallow, hurtling from the sky, dived at its traditional enemy. Zooming up and turning again, the swallow made another dive. This time its angry chatter brought another swallow. Now there were two attackers. Snippy fled in alarm. He flew up into a limb about ten feet above our heads. I called to him, but he was too busy watching the swallows. He didn't even notice the tidbits I threw out on the grass. Before we could make another move, Bluey flew up beside him. Now other birds were gathering: a pair of robins that had a nest in a neighboring spruce, a Baltimore oriole, two red-eyed vireos. They set up a clamor and scolded the jays, though none of them had worked up the courage to come within pecking distance. At each moment the crowd of birds increased.

Now I was alarmed. While Peg and the children called and tossed bits of food, I ran to the garage for the ladder. Perhaps if I put it gently against the branch, I could scare away the other birds and catch the jays before they flew still higher.

I was only halfway to the garage, however, when Peg called. "There they go!" she shouted.

I looked back to see the two jays flying off down the river. Behind them trailed a retinue of chattering, screaming birds. We ran out to the bridge and watched helplessly.

The robins and swallows that had started it all returned triumphantly to their nests, but there was no turning back for the jays. As they flew headlong, one after another of the birds nesting below rose to meet them. With no home territory to call their own, my two blue pets were outcasts. They had no place to turn to escape their tormentors.

"Oh, Lord," I said aloud as we watched the flock grow smaller until it looked like a swarm of gnats in the distance, "don't let them get separated."

But almost as I spoke the words, the swarm divided. One group continued onward, but the other faltered. Then, ominously, it descended to earth.

Rushing to the car, I sped across the bridge and down the road. If one of the jays had fallen, perhaps I could rescue him before it was too late. But when I got to the spot where I thought he had come down, there was not a sound. He was either dead or hiding. The smaller birds were already back about their business. I called and poked around through the bushes, but found no trace of him.

Returning to the car, I could just hear the cries of the other birds. Finally I saw them, but there was little I could do. The friendless second jay was up in the top of a dead elm. Near him perched six or eight birds. His usually jaunty cap was pressed down close to his head, his wings hung loosely, and his beak was open as he panted for breath. Every move he made was attended by a new clamor from the birds around him.

I watched in helpless futility for perhaps a quarter of an hour. He flew from one part of the tree to another, but there was no sanctuary. Finally he took off again, this time straight toward the wooded hill which flanks the west bank of the valley.

Now the chatter of the birds was joined by a new sound—the scream of a member of his own kind. For a moment my hopes rose, but in an instant they were dashed. Driving toward the tired little jay with vindictive wingbeats came two of his wild relatives. Doubtless sensing a threat to their own territory from this unknown invader, they hurled themselves on him, scattering the smaller birds.

And there, against the dark green of the spruces and the lighter hues of the beeches and maples, three flecks of blue appeared and disappeared through the branches. Finally all was quiet. The two wild jays winged homeward. They'd defended their territory against the youthful intruder who'd made the fatal blunder of flying right toward their home. Bluey and Snippy—strangers in their native land—had been given their freedom.

This is why we don't cage our creatures. They don't learn to be absolutely dependent on man. And, when they're ready, they return to the wild at their own speed. Our squirrels, Sparky and Lady Furry-tail, took three or four weeks to make the transition. They'd come back to the porch for nuts and sun-flower seeds daily, acting a bit more furtive each time. Finally both of them took to the tops of our big sugar maples. We still get glimpses of them, though, so we know they've reverted safely to the wild.

Then there were our two chipmunks. When their mother was killed by a cat, the feline's contrite owner brought the tiny orphans to me. They were so small that I could cradle both of them in one cupped hand. They were naked and blind, but hungry and eager to live. We fed them with a medicine dropper until they were big enough to go off on their own.

The chipmunks gradually returned to their natural element, although they never really made the final break. They couldn't forget the kitchen in which they were raised. For two summers now, an unsuspecting friend, visiting our home, would see a little striped rodent force the screen door open, steal a few sunflower seeds from a dish in the corner, and dart away again.

So we knew from previous experience that we weren't going to be able to let our cactus-critter go, just like that. And in the meantime we decided to learn as much about him as we could. Since human memory is faulty at best, I left a pad and pencil on a windowsill of the porch. Then I instructed the family to jot down any worthwhile observations.

The notations are interesting. Here are a few:

"Piney *can* throw his quills, but by mistake. Whirled and hit the leg of the porch sofa with his tail. Quill must have been loose—it flew about two feet."

"His front feet are like hands with four fingers and no thumb. He can curl his fingers like us. He can curl his palm from side to side, too. We can't do that."

"Piney smells like a pineapple."

"Smells more like orange peel."

"Smells good anyway."

"Piney can get a good grip. The skin of his hands looks as if it was covered with hundreds of little suction cups. He held so tight to the medicine dropper that the bulb came off when I tried to pull it away."

"June 14. He is beginning to eat solid food. Today he tried to eat my camera."

"Donald Brown says porcupines eat grass sometimes. Tried him on grass. All he did was climb up my sleeve and nibble my ear."

"Maybe you've got a grassy ear."

"He *loves* whole wheat bread. Doesn't like plain white bread. We ought to tell Justin Brande." (Justin is a friend who's an ardent advocate of natural foods. He even grinds his own whole wheat flour.)

"But he loves candy, too. I'm going to tell Dr. Murray." (Chandler Murray is our dentist.)

"Piney ate the pencil" (written in ink).

"He weighs two pounds on our bathroom scale. June 23."

"I haven't heard him click his teeth at all lately." (When we first got him, his teeth would chatter rapidly whenever he was nervous or frightened.)

"A baby porcupine is a porcupet. At least ours is."

There were a number of intriguing things about our "porcupet" which I learned only in due time. I wondered, for instance, just which of his senses he employed to compensate for his feeble eyesight. After all, if he got away from his tree, say, at the edge of the forest, what would prevent him from wandering out into the fields?

There were several answers. In the first place he didn't need to leave the tree until he was good and ready. The clinging power of Piney's feet was phenomenal. It often took two people to pry him loose from his perch. One person pulled gently, holding him carefully by the front limbs. The other would unfasten his hind feet—one toe at a time. And, like as not, just as one foot got unclamped, Piney would manage to grab hold again. It would take a hurricane to dislodge a grip like that.

Then, too, we realized, even a porky's bleary eyes can tell light from dark. The open sky of a meadow is different from the darker outlines of a forest, so he can keep his bearings. And Mother Nature, apparently repenting for shortchanging him visually, put his eyes on the sides of his head. Thus he can see the entire fuzzy horizon at one sweep—even if it is mainly peopled by gray ghosts.

One book in my library told of a hiker who came across a porcupine on the ground in the woods. The quill-pig hadn't noticed him, so the man stood perfectly still to see what the animal would do. To his surprise, the myopic creature walked right up to his leg and started to nibble his boot!

With weak eyes, apparently, come keen ears. This is frequently true even with humans. A friend of mine has been blind since childhood; his hearing is incredible. He can tell if a door is open in a room, for instance, by the difference in the echo from the walls. He can "hear" a building, or even a tree, probably in the same way.

We don't know whether Piney employed his hearing this way or not, but there was little doubt that it was keen. We could not sneak up on him without being detected. This, of course, may have been due to the slight vibration of our footsteps. Even the click of a doorlatch made him snap to attention.

His sense of smell was helpful, too. That blunt, black nose was frequently in motion. We'd often hear Piney snuffling when there was something nearby that he didn't understand. Usually he'd lose interest after a few whiffs. Apparently his nose had told him what his eyes didn't know. And after he'd finished his bread or cookies, he'd go around the floor like a vacuum cleaner until he'd found every crumb.

Then there was that tail. Stout and muscular, it was able to probe like some kind of oversized finger. Roger said it reminded him of a rear-mounted antenna. Piney was almost as good at going backward as he was at moving forward. Whenever he backed up he'd feel his way minutely with his tail, exploring every bump and crevice. So I suppose, if he couldn't see exactly what was ahead, he could always turn around and back his way into it.

The biggest counterbalance to 3/20 vision, however, was simply this: he just plain didn't need to see any better. After all, when you can saunter through life finding that nearly everything is edible—while you yourself can't be eaten—what is there to see, anyway?

The natural history of the porcupine seems to prove the point. In reading up on our engaging little boarder, I discovered that his ancestors may have bungled their way through North America as long as two million years ago. They could well have waddled right under the noses of great bears, mammoths, and the saber-toothed tiger. And this, as Peg said, is pretty good for not knowing where you're going.

Those quills, which served Piney's ancestors so faithfully, are actually modified hairs. They are just one example of the number of themes nature can play on a single string. Many animals, porcupines included, employ their whiskers as delicate organs of touch. The Florida manatee uses its pencil-sized feelers to locate the aquatic plants on which it feeds. Legend says that Columbus mistook these placid sea cows for mermaids, though I can't imagine even a lovelorn sailor snuggling up to that bristly harelip.

The luxuriant fur of the silver fox protects it against the Arctic cold, if not against man. The hoofs of my horses show their hairy origin by the fibrous nature of their bases. Our fingernails are first cousins to our hair, too.

As we inspected Piney's exterior we could see that his coat showed a great deal of variation. The hair on his belly was soft and short. Along his sides, legs, and face it became coarser. On his back its stiffness and length increased. Many of the hairs were semi-quills; they came to a point, with the same backward-pointing scales along the tip that form the "barbs" of the quill.

The actual quills were like the central shaft of a feather, although scarcely larger around than the lead of a pencil. Piney's small needles seldom exceeded an inch in length, but I've seen four-inch spikes on his twenty-pound relatives in our woods. His Asiatic and tropical cousins may boast eighteen-inch spears.

Since porkies wander through most of the northern United States and Canada, they keep blundering into dogs, cats, and domestic animals. My Vermont neighbors come in for their share of such woes. Some farm dogs never seem to learn. They attack every porcupine they meet. Then, with a faceful of quills, they come mournfully home to be de-stickered.

There are a number of suggested ways to remove porky quills. "Soak them in vinegar," one neighbor will say to another as they survey a distracted pup. "It'll soften them so they'll be easier to pull out."

A second neighbor swears by lemon juice; still another by tomato juice. There are also the olive oil school, the grape juice fraternity, and the warm milk association.

One old 'coonhunter in Starksboro suggested that the offending stickers be slathered liberally with whiskey. "It may not make the quills come out any easier," he admitted, "but at least the dog'll be happy."

Then, too, you can cut off the ends of the quills. The reasoning is that they will collapse because they are hollow and they can thus be drawn out more easily. I've yet to see a truly hollow quill, however. I have some before me at the moment; they're filled with a white pithy substance somewhat like styrofoam. I sliced them in two with a razor blade some time ago, and they don't look as if they've changed a bit since.

I think the best and most direct approach to the removal of quills is pulling them out with a pair of pliers. Or bundle the dog off to some lucky veterinarian and give him the job.

After those first few days, however, we seldom had to face such problems with Piney. Although his technical name—*Erethizon dorsatum*—means "the irritable back," he apparently didn't understand Latin. As a young visitor said after petting him: "He's not a porcupine. He's just Piney."

Just the same, we all managed to get quilled. The little fellow treated each of us like a walking obstacle course. If we came within range of those rounded, half-hidden ears, that keen nose, or those bleary eyes, he'd do all in his power to reach us. Then he'd try to climb.

If we picked him up, he'd clamber all over our arms and shoulders, grunting his recognition call as he investigated. Or, if we were wearing trousers or slacks, we'd allow him to start the climb up from the floor on his own. He'd talk all the way up: hunh, hunh, hunh. And often, after we had set him down again, we'd discover that a spine or two had caught in our clothing.

Sometimes it'd be hours before we discovered Piney's contribution. Working deeper with each movement, the quill would penetrate layers of clothing until it finally reached the skin. At that point, it would usually scratch enough to be noticed.

Occasionally a quill would work its way into the flesh without being felt at all. The skin is laced with tiny nerve endings which feel heat, cold, pain, and so on, but the point of a quill is so sharp that it may strike a space between the nerve endings and produce no feeling. Even when it does hurt, the pain is slight. The slender needlelike point touches only a few nerve endings at best.

I recall scratching a "mosquito bite" on my arm one night after retiring. Then I discovered that the cause of the itch was not a mosquito at all, but a deeply embedded quill. It had worked itself nearly a quarter-inch into my arm before I even noticed it.

One day after Piney had climbed around my shoulders for a while, I decided he'd had enough. Piney, however, was of a different opinion. He clung tightly to my shirt as I tried to pull him away. Then just as I relaxed my hold for a better grip, so did the porcupine. Result: (1) he lost his footing; (2) without thinking, I reached out and grabbed him; (3) I hastily set him down again; and (4) Peg pulled nearly two dozen quills out of my hands.

Maybe they didn't hurt going in, but coming out was another story because then their barbed points caught in the flesh. I could immediately sympathize with the thousands of bears, wolves, bobcats, and mountain lions that had found out about porcupines through a bad case of the miseries.

We learned continuously from our brambly pet. He reminded some people of the old-world hedgehog. In Europe I had seen these small, active mammals as they trotted about in search of insects, frogs, and fruit. Although the two animals aren't related, there is a certain similarity. To many of my neighbors a porky is a hedgehog, and that's that. The squirrel-sized hedgehog, however, has no barbs on its spines. To defend itself, it rolls up in a silent ball instead of swatting at the enemy with its tail. And it often lives in hedges (hence the name) while porkies, of course, live in trees.

Our deadpan comedian could walk along a limb upside down as easily as he could in any other position. We were also sure he could swim, and one day he proved it.

"Dad," sighed Alison after she'd worked fifteen minutes trying to feed Piney when all he wanted to do was get on her shoulder, "he's all sticky and messy. I got milk all over him."

I looked at my frustrated daughter. The porcupine had playfully allowed most of the milk to trickle down his chin and legs. "Well," I joked, "why don't you give him a bath?"

"In the tub?"

"No. Make it easy on yourself. Take him down to the river."

She chuckled. It was a warm day, and the prospect of a dip in that river in front of the house had a certain appeal.

Enamored by my own suggestion, I decided to go along. Holding Piney at arm's length in spite of his attempts to climb to my shoulder, I rushed down the bank to the edge of the river. Storing him in a small bush for a moment, we quickly took off our shoes and socks.

Extracting Piney from the bush, I waded out sev- eral feet from shore where he couldn't possibly touch bottom. "Okay, Piney," I said, setting him adrift, "sink or swim."

As far as I knew, he'd never been in the water be- fore. But, like most animals, he had all the swim- ming ability he needed. He moved along in a fine dog paddle.

Actually, he needn't have known how to swim at all. Every one of those airy quills served to buoy him up. I've heard of people who floated like a cork, but Piney *was* a cork. All two and a half pounds of him bobbed around as if he was wearing a life preserver. And so he was—several thousand of them.

He splashed around until he was thoroughly rinsed. I even ducked him a couple of times to wet his head. He didn't approve completely, but man- fully struggled along until we hauled him back to dry land. Once on shore, he stood on what Alison calls his "tripod"—hind legs and tail—and shook himself like a dog.

"There," said Alison. "That's what you get for messing with your food."

Piney had several other methods of entertaining himself besides playing with his food. One of his favorites was what we called his war dance. In performing this feat, he'd whirl in a circle, stiff-legged, with quills raised. Then slashing his tail back and forth, he'd run forward a few steps, spin several times, and then run backward. Sometimes he'd grunt a challenge at an unseen foe. More often he'd dance in silence. Occasionally we'd turn on the porch light, long after dark, and find our porcupine dancing in the center of the floor.

A second game was what Peg called "midnight canteen." She had hung an old Girl Scout canteen on a hook above the porch table several years ago. There, long forgotten, it dangled by its strap. Piney, however, soon found it.

He informed us of his discovery late one night. We'd been asleep an hour or two when an unusual sound woke us up. Bump-bump. Bump-bump.

"What's going on downstairs?" Peg asked.

Quietly we went downstairs and turned on the light. There was our small insomniac, having a wrestling match with the canteen. He was absorbed in his game, and didn't notice the light at all. He'd pull the canteen away from the wall, hold it in his two arms, and tuck his chin down over it as tightly as possible. Then he'd back away until the strap pulled it out of his grasp. "Bump" went the canteen, followed almost instantly by Piney's version of a charging porcupine. Then "bump," as he crashed into it and grabbed it again.

Apparently this was more fun than anything. And, for a creature far more active by night than by day, what better time than at 2:40 in the morning?

In spite of our grumbles, neither of us suggested banishing the bumps by removing the canteen. This, I suppose, just points out how a porcupine can get under your skin.

Piney loved to wrestle, too. He thrashed his teddy bear all over the porch. And when we gave him a small broom with a broken handle, he picked it up, carried it a few feet in his teeth, and shook it like a dog. As with "midnight canteen," Piney found such antics were best enjoyed after dark—preferably when we were all asleep.

Another of his games was even more conducive to a good night's rest. Most rodents gnaw almost constantly because their teeth never stop growing. Gnawing helps keep them sharp and trimmed. Once I saw a squirrel skull which had one of the upper incisors missing. Its mate in the lower jaw, lacking anything to grind against, had grown into a great, curving tusk. Finally it had arched around and penetrated the brain.

Piney's gnawing, however, seemed to be for another purpose. From what we could figure out, he liked the sound of the porch being gnawed. All of it.

He didn't really chew on such things. He just nibbled. He did all his serious chewing, thank heaven, in his birch tree. The doorsill had a fine deep tone, due perhaps to the hollowness of the floor beneath. Piney discovered how to nip away at it without really harming a thing, "crunch, crunch, crunch." Then, like as not, he'd make his way up to a certain window near the southeast corner and pull repeatedly at a loose strip of the casing, "snap, snap, snap."

Since our old porch is not really square at any point, there was a piece of wallboard that gaped a bit at the lower corner. Piney could elicit a resounding "thunk" by grasping it with his teeth, pulling it slightly, and then releasing it. We managed to get used to his noises, however, so I was a bit surprised one night when Peg woke me with a jab in the ribs. "Now what's that porcupine doing?" she asked.

I listened for a moment. "Woodwork concerto," I quipped, proud of myself for giving such a clever answer after being awakened from a sound sleep. "By a porcupine, it'd have to be in A-sharp . . ."

She jabbed me again. "All right, all right. You can quit laughing at your own jokes. If that's a woodwork concerto, who's got the guitar?"

I listened once more. Twang. Then silence. Then twang again.

Downstairs we went. Turning on the light, we peered out onto the porch.

Piney's tree had bent over far enough to allow him to get his feet on the casing of the screen door. From that point, with a firm hold on the branches, he could just reach the top of the door. By grasping the top, he could pull the door far enough to stretch the spring that held it shut. And there he was, plunking away at the spring by pulling on the door and letting it snap back in place—half in an attempt to climb on the door and half in what seemed to be an obvious enjoyment of the sound.

"All right," I told our midnight maestro as I righted the tree, "show's over. Here's a piece of chocolate. Now, for heaven's sake, let us sleep."

All of this is just part of the game when you have a porcupine. It was pretty good, we agreed, when a potential woodland tragedy turned out to be something that was so much fun.

Well, maybe not fun exactly, at three A.M. But different, anyway.

Until Piney got used to his new family, he had to be handled with care.

Here, Piney investigates the Rood's bird bath.

Piney proudly demonstrates his ability to go out on a limb.

Above left, Piney snuggles up to his teddy bear.
Above right, Piney does his fireman act on the kitchen chair.
Below, a thoughful Piney chews on a slice of whole wheat bread.

Piney, shown here with author Ronald Rood, was a most affectionate pet.

4

VISITORS

"DAD, there's a car outside."

"All right, Roger. Just a minute." I had to see what Snoopy was up to in today's paper.

"But, Dad. I think it's the police."

I dropped Snoopy, doghouse and all. "The *who?*"

"The police. He's getting out of his car."

I looked out the window. A green sedan, complete with red light on top, occupied our driveway. Usually our noisy bridge tells us of impending visitors. We call it our fifty-foot doorbell. But this time we hadn't noticed the sound. At any rate, there he was—as unexpected as if he'd dropped from another planet.

I took a quick mental inventory. What on earth did he want? As far as I knew, my fifteen-year-old son had never done anything worse than get a "D" on a report card. I couldn't imagine a policeman having any business with Peg or Alison, either—except perhaps if one of them had run a stop sign by mistake. Janice, our older daughter, was thirty miles away, teaching at a special school in Brandon. Our son Tom was just starting a hitch at an air base in Delaware. As for myself, I doubted if any of my own childhood deeds were catching up with me at this late date.

Probably our official visitor merely wanted to pass the time of day. So I sauntered over to him.

A closer look, however, revealed that he was not a policeman. He was a game warden. And it wasn't the time of day he had on his mind.

He got right to the point. "Mr. Rood, seems that I recall reading something you once wrote about not keeping wild animals in captivity."

"That's right. Makes 'em dependent on people—"

"It's also against the law."

"But this is just a little—"

"Little ones grow up to be big ones. People don't very often catch full-grown game animals for pets. They start with them while they're young. They're cute, and everybody's happy. But then they grow up. They're still wild animals, but with no fear of man. First thing you know, somebody gets hurt. And somebody complains."

I knew, of course, that Vermont, like many other states, wisely frowned on keeping game animals in captivity. All sorts of heinous deeds had been perpetrated in the name of sport.

I knew of a batch of ducks, for instance, that had been trained to fly every night from a raised platform in order to find their supper at a distant feeding point. Thus they made perfect wing shots for "sportsmen" who didn't even have to bother to hide. I had also heard of the vicious practice of raising raccoons as "bait." Tied to a log in a pond, they were set upon by dogs until they were drowned or torn to bits.

But even the muskrats we'd once had in the cellar hadn't really been confined. They'd been free to go out the hatchway door, which had purposely been left open. In fact, they finally left by this very route.

During our conversation we had been standing outside the front porch, and Piney chose this moment to push something over. It dropped with a little thud. My visitor tilted his head in the direction of the sound. "Is he in there? On the porch?"

I nodded.

"Looks to me like he's confined. You've got a game animal in captivity."

"No. That's the whole point. I'm *not* keeping a game animal in captivity. All I've done is rescue a—"

But he didn't seem to be listening. Mounting the steps, he peered cautiously through a porch window. He looked for a minute, then turned to me.

His face bore an expression of bewilderment.

"—a porcupine," he said, finishing my sentence for me. "A baby porcupine. They sent me all the way out here for a porcupine."

"Piney's his name," I added helpfully.

He knitted his brows. "You've got no bear cub?"

"Good heavens, no!"

Now we both began to see the humor of it. Somehow, Piney had turned into a cub of Vermont's most impressive game animal—the black bear. Perhaps I'd mentioned to someone that we had a "cub" without identifying it as a little porky. Or possibly someone had been driving by and had seen Piney out on the lawn with us. After all, he was black and round like a little bear.

This, then, was the reason for the official visit. The rule, after all, stated that thou shalt not possess, keep, confine, or restrict any game bird or animal out of season. And since this was July instead of December, it was definitely out of season. For bears, at least.

But not for porcupines. A porky was different. He could hardly be called a game animal. His destructive habits have resulted in a price being placed on his head. So, far from it being against the law to interfere with a porcupine in the Green Mountain State, it's often regarded as highly commendable. As late as 1953 Vermont porkies were the subject of a bounty.

The whole business of bounties has been a hot potato ever since rewards for "varmints" were established by our infant nation. One of New York's first acts as a sovereign state nearly two hundred years ago was to set up a wild-animal bounty. Other states soon followed suit.

In the case of the porcupine, it was often necessary to surrender a pair of ears to a town clerk. That solemn official then recorded your good fortune and dutifully paid a quarter or so for the privilege of tossing your offering into a "bounty box." Sometimes the box was emptied into the trash can in back, from which enterprising youngsters would remove the ears and bring them to the front door again. And it is known that a trapper with a steady hand could cut as many as a dozen pairs of "ears" from the belly of a single porcupine.

To help keep people honest, the state sometimes required the presentation of tails. This was a popular way to collect a reward for foxes. You could not easily manufacture a tail from another portion of the skin. Besides, the surrender of a tail was pretty good proof that you had had a fox in hand. But even this requirement had its drawbacks. One could catch a fox, cut off its tail, and let it go—to raise six or eight tailed young in a single year. No sense, the bounty hunters agreed, in killing the goose that laid the golden egg.

It didn't do much good, either, to surrender the whole animal to the proper authority for payment.

In more than one instance, the proper authority turned out to be not so proper. He merely took the noisome carcasses to another person and collected a little money for himself on the side. Then, too, a brisk carcass trade developed across the border from a nonbounty state to one with looser purse strings.

Of course, with the porcupine, as with other animals who seem to oppose man's interests, we seldom stop to make one basic admission: he was here first.

Since my uniformed visitor had found that Piney's case required no official action, I brought Piney out for inspection. The little fellow proceeded to win him over completely. He climbed the gray-green sleeve, tried to nibble the stiff-brimmed hat, and grunted wheezy nothings in the official ear.

Finally, after we'd swapped porcupine yarns for half an hour, the warden drove away. "But I'll stop in again," he grinned. "I've got to get a picture of this with my camera. They'll never believe me if I don't."

In a way, his visit was typical. The porcupine is so strongly etched in the public imagination that people just have to see him for themselves. After all, if a porcupine can travel safely even under the nose of a grizzly bear, it must be a formidable animal, indeed. So, as news of Piney spread, we had more visitors.

One, like the warden, came to wag an admonishing finger for our mistreatment of a wild animal. Happily, when she saw our myopic little forester sniffing companionably from the top of his tree, she was persuaded that there was no mistreatment here. Another, with fire in his eye, came to give us his opinion of anybody who'd give shelter to anything as useless as a pesky "hedgehog." Piney won him over, too.

Most visitors, however, came not out of principle but out of a sense of curiosity. Some of them were total strangers. These might be people who had merely been out for a Sunday drive, and had stopped in Lincoln to ask directions. In the process of asking "what is there to see around here, anyway?" they'd been informed about Piney. Within a few minutes, we'd have a carload of visitors.

"Wonder if we could take a picture of your porcupine," they'd ask as they disembarked from the car, camera in hand. So we'd obligingly extract Piney from the porch. Then, after introductions all around, we'd pose, they'd pose, and Piney would end up in another photo album.

We hadn't had our porcupine a month before Fletcher and Hattie Brown appeared. Fletcher's farm is up beyond ours; the common fence line which we share passes near the pond and continues through the maples of our sugar woods. In the spring, he taps these sugar maples for their sap and boils it down into syrup and sugar.

For years he used the old buckets and the picturesque gathering rig which have been so much a part of rural Vermont. Now, however, he inserts small plastic spouts in the holes drilled in the maple trunks each spring. From these he runs a maze of quarter-inch plastic tubing through the woods. The sap runs through the tubes to a central storage tank, and from there to his sugar house.

Even with modern equipment, it's a hard job. It requires days to take the plastic pipe through the deep snow and hitch it to the trees. And once you've collected the sap, as many as forty gallons of it must be boiled down to make a single gallon of syrup.

Porcupines, with that sweet tooth and their craving for salt from sweaty hands, don't make it any easier, either. They chew Fletcher's tubing during sugaring season, allowing the sap to run uselessly out on the snow. They attack the tires of his tractor if it stands overnight in the woods. And when sugaring season is over, they nibble artistic holes in the sugar house. Wandering around inside, they sample a door handle here, a window frame there.

So, even though Fletcher and Hattie have a deep love for their native Vermont and its living things, they have a hard time justifying the porcupine.

Thus the Browns viewed Piney in his little domain on the porch with unbridled amazement. When I pointed out that he didn't chew doors and windows because he probably got enough salt and sugar in his bread and cookies, Fletcher shook his head.

"First you had raccoons," he said. "Then skunks. Then woodchucks and squirrels, and now this porcupine. All I can say is that it's lucky we don't have rattlesnakes around here."

Then there were our camping friends. Our yard provides plenty of room for an overflow in case weekend visitors cannot all be accommodated in the house. If the weather is fair, we sometimes put cots right out on the lawn for kids who feel like roughing it. We have a tent, too, plus a small shed which we've converted into a cabin. Visiting children love to stay overnight in the cabin. They clutch the covers in delicious terror as an owl hoots in the darkness—until the murmur of the river lulls them to sleep.

Bill and Judy Peterson arrived in a station wagon with a load of kids. They were old friends, and the doors of the wagon burst open almost before it had come to a full stop. In a moment, children were everywhere.

They were on their way to Montreal and hoped we'd be home for an overnight visit.

"You know what they say," quipped Judy. " 'Summer in Vermont is when distant relatives are no longer distant.' But here are some hot dogs and watermelon to help ease the strain—"

Her words were interrupted by a furious barking. "Rebel!" I shouted.

"Duchess!" called Bill.

"Piney!" gasped Peg.

We hadn't noticed their cocker spaniel. She must have jumped from the car as soon as the door opened.

Sniffing her way around, she had come to the porch with its tantalizing smell of porcupine. Apparently the door wasn't fully latched, and she'd been able to push it open. Now she stood inside, calling Piney names at the top of her doggy voice. Rebel, who was inside the house, shouted encouragement.

"Oh, no!" I gasped as I sprinted for the porch. "Does Duchess know about porcupines?"

Without waiting for an answer, I thrust open the door. Piney was in the top of his tree, bristled to twice his size and looking down at the frenzied Duchess. She pranced around at the bottom, daring him to come down and fight like a man—or at least like a dog.

Thank heavens it wasn't too late. I thought of what a mouthful of quills could do to a beautiful friendship.

Bill shooed the excited Duchess outside. Then, letting Rebel out to keep her company, we introduced Piney all around. The children were delighted with him at once, but Bill and Judy pretended to have their reservations.

"They've kept us awake all night," Bill recalled. "They grunt and talk all the time. And they'll chew anything. One night in Michigan they gnawed the ropes of our tent so that the whole side fell in."

"And don't forget the TV dinners, either," Judy said. "They'll bite right through that aluminum. And they'll chew a hole in a carton of milk. Ask us.

We know from experience. What a mess!"

I pointed out that Piney was above such tricks. "Why, he's no more trouble," I assured them, "than a pet rabbit."

But our "rabbit" held another trump card. In fact, he'd already played it. Little JoAnne was the one to discover it.

"Daddy," she said, "what's wrong with Duchess?"

We looked out the porch window. The cocker spaniel was going through some highly unspaniel-like behavior. She pawed frantically at her muzzle with her front feet. Then she put her snout down into the grass and pushed ahead like a black little bulldozer. She got up and ran in a circle. Then she sat down abruptly and dug at her nose again.

Rebel, not knowing what it was all about, tried to play with her, but she snapped at him. Bill called, but she seemed not to hear. By the time we got out to the poor creature, she was trying to bury herself under the lilac bush.

Bill squatted down and put his arms around the miserable little dog. She whined and tried to hide her head against his side. He grasped her chin in his hands and forced it up so that he could look at her. There were perhaps a dozen quills in her muzzle.

My heart sank.

"Must have got in touch with Piney before he ran up his tree," I observed, for lack of anything better to say. "She's just beginning to feel the quills."

Bill and Judy murmured agreement. Then I heard Peg turn and go back to the house. In a moment she returned with those thick leather ski gloves and a pair of pliers.

I gave Bill his choice of the pliers or the gloves. He took the gloves.

So, while Judy held the rear portion of Duchess and Bill forced her mouth open with the gloves, I extracted nearly two dozen needles from the nose and mouth of the downtrodden spaniel.

We were getting to be experts at this, I ruefully told myself. First Rebel, and now Duchess about five weeks later. Thank heavens it had been Bill and Judy. Good friends that they were, they just laughed the whole thing off. Duchess took it in good grace, too, and was playing with Rebel within half an hour. But she wouldn't go near the porch again.

"Besides," Bill said the next morning as they packed the last of their belongings and piled into the car, "what else are friends for?"

And waving the little packet of quills they'd saved as a memento, they escaped to Montreal.

"At least," said Peg, as the sound of their station wagon receded, "they *know* their souvenirs were made in Vermont."

About a week after Piney's introduction to Duchess, an elderly man and woman, whom we knew slightly, drove up in the rain.

"My husband's got to see someone for a few minutes up in South Lincoln," announced the woman, whom we'll call Mrs. Jones. "So I thought I'd stop in 'til he came back. If it's all right, that is."

Peg hastily assured her that it was fine. I'd been sorting photographs on the kitchen table, so I gathered them up and made a hasty exit to the next room, leaving the field to the ladies. Spreading the pictures out again on the table, I continued my work against the background of feminine conversation in the other room.

After a few minutes, I hardly blamed Mr. Jones for wanting to head for South Lincoln alone. Living two miles away from town, we were not up on the latest gossip. But Peg was given a very liberal education in the next half hour—very liberal, indeed— about a good portion of the town's population.

Mrs. Jones had just gotten wound up when I heard our "doorbell" rumble. Glancing out, I saw that it was her husband. It was raining so hard that he sat waiting in the car. As she stood with her hand on the doorknob, she let us in on a few more juicy bits such as the comparison of the town's birthrate with the marriage rate. Then, with the interesting observation that a member of my own women's chorus might wear a wig "and something else that isn't hers either," she opened the door.

Still talking, she reached down for her umbrella. But then her voice trailed off in midsentence. With a little yelp, she backed into the kitchen. "What sort of a creature is that?" she gasped.

"Just Piney," I volunteered. "Our porcupine."

"Porcupine!"

"Sure. I'll show you. He's a nice little fellow."

I reached down to pick him up, but as I put my hands under his arms to lift him, I realized something was amiss.

Not amiss, exactly. Wrong.

Piney was taking his ease in the middle of what looked like a pile of soap chips. But they weren't soap chips at all. They were scraps of ivory. Of all the times he could have chosen, Piney had picked this moment to remind us that he was only partly domesticated. The rest was still wild porcupine. And to prove it, he had nibbled Mrs. Jones' antique ivory umbrella handle into a sculpture all his own.

"I guess he's been chewing your umbrella," I observed brightly. "Gosh, I'm terribly sorry. We'll get you another?"

I couldn't help but put a question mark at the end of the sentence. The look she gave me demanded it. But her expression also gave me the answer. Obviously there *was* no other. For all I knew, that umbrella was a gift with a charter membership in the Colonial Dames.

"No," she said firmly, "no. It's my fault for leaving the umbrella out on the porch. I should have known better." And she flounced out, holding her umbrella imperiously by all that was left of the handle.

I looked at Peg. "Now what did she mean, 'I should have known better'?"

My wife's voice was calm, but there was a smile in it, too. "Ronald," she said with elaborate seriousness, "if you don't know what she meant by this time, you'll never know at all."

"Well," I countered lamely, "he's your porcupine, too."

I looked down at Piney. He was nosing around in the chips, perhaps searching for some morsel he'd missed. I reached down and picked him up by his front legs.

"You little dickens," I said, holding him so his black nose nearly touched mine and his watery navy-blue eyes could take in my disapproving scowl, "what on earth's getting into you? First it's the Petersons' dog and now it's Mrs. Jones' umbrella. One of these days somebody's going to take a club to you. They'll swat you right into the middle of next week. And we'll be minus one porcupine."

This was a thought. If anybody was going to approach our porcupine with murder in his eye, perhaps something should be done. "You know," I said to Peg as I put Piney down and gave him a fig bar, "perhaps we'd better find out about porcupine insurance."

Peg looked at me. *"For* him, dear," she said, "or *against* him?"

5

Now THAT we were in July, we had another head-
ache. It was none of Piney's doing, but he was involved. It concerned the pony swim.

Five years ago we'd taken Roger and Alison for a
camping vacation along Virginia's Atlantic shore.
We'd planned it for late July so as to coincide with
one of the East's most unusual spectacles—the annual
roundup and auction of the famous wild ponies at
Chincoteague, Virginia.

Nobody knows exactly how those tough little
horses happened to be on the Virginia coast in the
first place. Their ancestors may have been ship-
wrecked there on a trip from Spain to the New
World. Perhaps they are the only remnant of a settle-
ment of colonists which died out, leaving no other
trace.

At any rate, there they are, on the island of Assateague, a narrow sandbar separated from Chincoteague by a tidal channel.

Scarcely a mile wide at its broadest point, Assateague stretches from Ocean City, Maryland, along the brink of the Atlantic Ocean to Chincoteague, some thirty-three miles to the south. Most of the ponies live at its southern tip, among loblolly pines, dune grass, bayberries, beach heather, and other plants that manage to survive in the sandy soil.

The ponies, of every pattern and color, wander picturesquely among the sand dunes of this wild land. Now scarcely the size of western cow ponies, they may have been larger originally. The rugged life they've led has probably tended to dwarf them. They roam through Assateague's salt marshes among the herons, egrets, ducks, geese, swans, and shorebirds which live there in such profusion that the air constantly throbs with the beat of their wings and the noise of their cries.

When the mosquitoes become too bad, the ponies make for the beach. Pounding toward the surf at a full gallop, they scatter terns, gulls, sanderlings, and skimmers as they head for the cooling water. Sometimes they plunge right into the breakers to rid themselves of the pesky insects.

The early settlers in Chincoteague soon availed themselves of the free horsepower that existed just a pony swim away. And as word of the hardy little steeds spread, the pony swim became a local attraction.

Some time later, the Chincoteague Volunteer Fire Department decided to put the swim on a money-making basis. The plan was to capture the ponies and sell the foals. This was also a good conservation practice since the narrow offshore bar could support just so many ponies. From this beginning sprang the annual two-week carnival. It is climaxed by a roundup, pony swim, and auction, sometimes called "the oldest wild West show in the East."

The idea turned out to be a gold mine. Each year, a day or so before the last Wednesday and Thursday of July, the two hundred wild ponies on Assateague are rounded up. A few are chased down with jeeps and sand buggies, but most of them are herded into a big corral by men on regular-sized horses which may be a quarter larger than their wild relatives. Each wild stallion has his harem of perhaps a dozen mares and their foals, and he forms them into little groups in the corral, biting and kicking if a male attempts to cut in.

On Wednesday morning the herd is released from its corral on Assateague and driven to the shore of the channel. When the tide is slack, the ponies are forced into the water. Even the smallest foals know how to swim, and they follow their mothers across the eighth-mile stretch to the shore of Chincoteague.

Many of the youngsters put their noses on their

mothers' rumps to help keep their heads out of the water. Some even hang onto the maternal tail with their teeth. When the animals gain the Chincoteague shore, they are quickly corralled again for the auction the following day.

It's an exciting time. For nearly two weeks the midway has been ablaze at night with its rides, souvenir stands, cotton candy, and guest performers. And there are plenty of those famous Chincoteague oyster sandwiches—actually oysters and batter, fried and served sizzling on a roll. Now, on that last Thursday in July, the scene shifts to the corral beneath the pines. There, for the first time, some fifty foals will feel the touch of human hands as they go to the highest bidders.

The fame of "pony penning" spreads each year. Although Chincoteague has little more than two thousand residents, the number swells tenfold for a few days. The air of gaiety, the friendliness of the people, and the spirit of an auction have a magical effect. Many a parent's firm "no!" has subsided into helpless acquiescence under the appeal of a wide-eyed youngster—and a wide-eyed foal—as the auctioneer chants the bids.

It had struck us that way, too. Roger had watched as little colts went for fifty, sixty, and seventy dollars. Finally, unable to stand it any longer, he had pressed seven dollars in my hand. It was all the money he had in the world.

But the look on his face made up the difference, and I impulsively nodded my approval. So he picked out the pony he liked and bid on it. Some ten minutes later I found myself paying sixty dollars with a lump in my throat and a fierce love for my son as he clasped his arms around his new pony.

After we bought him the four of us stood in a disorganized circle around Roger's animated trophy. We heard people congratulating us and telling us what a fine pony he was. At last we managed to collect ourselves enough to fashion a little wooden pen for him. Hoisting it into our station wagon, we put it in place. The next day, still a bit numb from the suddenness of the whole thing, we installed our pony. Then we began our triumphal return to Vermont with some fifty pounds of Virginia wildlife.

Very soon we discovered that Little Fellow, as Roger named him, had his own quirks. He preferred Peg's brambly rose bushes, for instance, to good green grass. He figured out the combination to the latch on the pasture gate, opened it, and went and stood in the river. He followed an indignant toad halfway across the pasture—his nose just an inch or two behind the portly creature—recoiling in surprise with every hop. He ate ice cream avidly and then stood around with his mouth open, trying to warm it up.

With such a bundle of personality out there on our north fourteen acres, we couldn't keep his story to ourselves. So, encouraged by my good friend Stephen Greene, who had published two of my previous books, I put Little Fellow's adventures down on paper. Now, with *Hundred Acre Welcome* hot off the press, Steve and I figured it would be a good idea to promote—and, hopefully, sell—copies of the book right at the pony auction where it had all started.

And this, of course, is where Piney came in. Or more correctly, where he'd have to be left out. Steve Greene had set up a schedule which involved visits to bookstores along the way. So we were going to have to start a couple of days early and work slowly south.

Then, too, Warren Conant, with whom we became friends at the time we bought the pony, had arranged for me to give a couple of talks in Chincoteague. Maybe we could tuck a porcupine away for a few hours, but how would we take care of him through two weeks of carnival and another pony auction?

No. Piney would have to stay home. Two weeks was far too long to have him with us. Somewhere we'd have to get a baby-sitter.

Actually we thought it would be easy to find someone. People had been so captivated with our juvenile quill-pig that we had had a number of offers to care for him. "Take him off your hands any time you'd like," Jim Welch had told me. Brad and Mary Cousino had said they'd be glad to have him, as had the Baileys.

So we sat out on the lawn one evening and determined which of our friends would be the fortunate ones. Finally we made our decision.

We went inside and I dialed a telephone number. "Bert," I said, "remember when you were up here a couple of weeks ago and we introduced you to our porcupine?"

"You bet, Ron. How's he doing?"

"Oh, he's fine. But we've got a problem. And we hoped maybe you could help."

"Sure. Anything I can do, just ask me."

"Well, it's this way. Peg and I have to go away in a couple of weeks for the rest of the month. And we thought we'd take you up on your offer to look after Piney while we were gone."

Silence. I glanced up at Peg. "Bert—you still there?"

"Um, yes." More silence.

"Do you think you could take him?"

"Well, uh, I dunno, Ron. The missus and I been thinking of taking off one of these weekends. To go— uh—visit my nephew. And it might just happen that we'd want to be away while you were gone."

"I wouldn't want that to happen, Bert. Just thought I'd ask—"

"But call me up the next time. Glad to help. Anytime."

I hung up and turned to Peg. "Says he's going to be away."

Probably he'd had enough experiences with porcupines on his farm to have a healthy respect for them. Well—there were plenty more people. So, on to the next.

My luck was better on the second try. Anne would be happy to take him. "But just a minute," she chirped, "I'll have to double-check with Frank. He's never met Piney, you know. He's on night shift now, so he'll be here all day while I'm at the furniture factory."

She laid the receiver down. I could hear her footsteps as she walked into the other room. Then there was a discussion.

Well, it was not exactly a discussion—more like an explosion. I heard something in the distance about "no damn hedgehog." Then there were footsteps once more. Anne was back on the phone again.

She cleared her throat. "Frank'd *love* to have him," she said enthusiastically. Then her voice sobered. "Only he's sort of busy right now. Going to start painting the kitchen next week."

She uttered the last statement in a raised tone of voice, no doubt for Frank's benefit. This might get the kitchen started, but it wasn't doing much for our porcupine.

Peg decided to try her luck. She called one of her fellow teachers, but he'd been thinking of taking a short summer course, and was considering a trip to Burlington the following day to see about it. Another teacher's mother wasn't feeling well, and might require a visit from her daughter at any time.

My wife put in one more call. After stating our request, she listened. And listened. She nodded sympathetically and murmured a dozen each of "yesses" and "noes." Then she hung up.

"What was their excuse?" I asked.

"Oh," she said airily, "Stan can't take any wild animals at all until at least a year from Tuesday. He's got dandruff."

This spoke eloquently of one thing anyway: even at two and a half pounds, the reputation of the porcupine is so formidable that people want nothing to do with him. Not for two whole weeks, anyway.

"Piney," I sighed, as I brought him in from the porch for supper, "looks as if you'd better wean yourself in the next week. Nobody wants a porcupine."

Still, there must be someone willing to care for our small pet. Of course, one of the problems was his need to be fed four times a day. He was doing better on bits of orange and whole wheat bread, but he still gulped the milk each time as if he hadn't eaten for a week.

Well, there was still a week to go. There must be somebody who: (1) didn't have a dog; (2) had the necessary room; (3) was able to take an hour a day, split into four periods, for feeding one small porcupine; and (4) was willing.

Over the next days we thought of a number of

people with all four qualifications. But the trouble was that none of them had all four at once.

Things were getting desperate. Here it was Tuesday already, and we were to leave for Chincoteague on Friday. One thing was sure: in spite of how much we cared for him, our small problem child couldn't go along.

We made more telephone calls. We found several people who would take him for a day or two, "but for two and a half weeks, Ron? Why don't you get somebody else?"

The trouble was that there wasn't "somebody else." Piney was a thorny problem, in more ways than one.

Until Wednesday when the reporter arrived.

He drove into our yard at about ten in the morning. Peg and I were shelling fresh peas at the picnic table on the lawn. Piney sat on the end of the table, holding a green pod in his paws, sampling it like a squirrel. He stopped for a moment when the car drove in, but his limited vision told him little. Sensing that we hadn't moved, he went back to nibbling.

The reporter was halfway out of his car when he discovered our porcupine. Without a word he ducked back inside again and emerged with a camera in hand. Looking at me questioningly, he asked wordlessly if he could take a picture. When I nodded, he clicked the shutter.

Piney bristled for a moment at the sound, but soon

went back to his salad. The photographer moved around, still saying nothing, until he had taken several more pictures. Finally he introduced himself.

"Mr. Rood? I'd like to do a story on your porcupine. What's his name?"

So it was that Piney met Mr. Sladen. And so it was, too, that our problem was solved. Mr. Sladen, half an hour after he'd been there, made it perfectly clear.

"Now, just a minute," he said, breaking in as I told him of my efforts to find a temporary home for Piney while we were away, "do you know why I came here?"

"To see the porcupine."

"Sure. And to get material for a story. I found out about him from a friend who saw him last week. Everybody's curious about porcupines."

"Well, they'll have to wait. We've got five bookstores to visit, and two talks to give, to say nothing of two weeks in a carnival booth."

"Oh, come on. Live it up. Take him with you."

"Take him with us! This trip is set up on a split-second schedule."

"So? What's a porcupine's time worth?"

He just didn't realize what he was saying. There were all kinds of complications. We'd traded the station wagon in for a sedan some time ago so where would we put Piney? In the back seat of the car? Even if we could fit him in somehow, what about his feeding schedule? Then there was the delicate question of sanitation. What do you do about that?

Furthermore, we planned to spend at least one night on the road, possibly two. I could just see the unbridled joy with which some motel owner in Philadelphia would greet a porcupine.

But my reporter friend shrugged off my objections. "How many people have come to see Piney since you've had him?"

"Oh, I don't know. Couple or three dozen. Maybe more."

"See? There you are. Most of them already know what a porcupine looks like, too. I'll bet I've seen a hundred, myself. Yet here I am. Boy, if I were you, I'd take little Piney, here, along with me. What better calling card do you want?"

Now Peg joined the conversation. "And who's going to clean up our nice back seat after we've had a porcupine in it for more than five hundred miles?"

"Get your husband to make him a cage. And take along plenty of newspapers to keep things in good shape. Everywhere you go, people will want to see him. Why, you could even charge admission. I bet they don't even know what a porcupine looks like down there. Doggone it, what can you lose?"

His enthusiasm began to take hold. Maybe it *was* a good idea. After all, if we'd brought fifty pounds of Chincoteague pony foal back to Vermont with us in our station wagon, forty ounces of porcupine ought to be easy. Besides, if this was a public relations jaunt, Piney might make a good agent, at that.

George Sladen was so convincing that I soon found myself reaching for my carpenter's rule. First we measured the back seat of the car. Then we measured an old wooden cage which had been brought to me some time before by a lady with a disgruntled squirrel. With trimming we could make it fit.

"There," said George as he got back into his car, "we've got her licked. Doggone if I don't wish I was going with you."

Peg smiled ruefully. "I wish you were, too."

"Oh, don't worry," he said. "You'll be glad you took him. Just wait and see. But don't forget those newspapers."

We watched as he yanked his car in gear and sped away, tossing twin streams of gravel all the way down the driveway. "And that," said Peg, "is what is known as the 'power of the press.'"

We had to admit that he'd offered a very convincing argument. Besides, there was another point in favor of his idea: we weren't going to find a nursemaid for Piney, anyway.

So we expanded our plans from a tour for two to a trip for three. Roger and Alison weren't going with us, because both had summer jobs, so we'd been referring to the vacation as our second honeymoon. Now, as Peg pointed out, it'd still be a honeymoon, but with a baby in the back seat.

We decided to call our friend, Warren Conant, down in Chincoteague. After all, they might like a couple of days to prepare themselves for Piney. But Warren and Pauline must have been in league with the reporter. They both thought it was a great idea, especially after I assured them there was no danger of Piney throwing any quills.

"Only one thing, Ron. Don't porcupines spend their lives up in the tops of trees? You'd better bring down a couple of branches so he won't be homesick."

After he'd hung up, we got to thinking about what he'd said. As long as we were going to have Piney with us anyway, we might as well make him comfortable.

In fact, as we thought more about it, it occurred to us that we might transform our carnival booth into a little corner of Vermont. If we got a lot of evergreens, and put Piney in the middle, we might have something that would make people look twice. And, if we worked at it, we might even have someone to talk to. Steve Greene was putting a lot into this book display. Maybe this would help the whole thing.

So Peg and I went up to the forest and each of us gathered a double armload of balsam fir. This durable evergreen is one of America's most aromatic trees. It is a favorite for Christmas trees and winter decorations, because its fragrance lasts for a long time. Even after the needles are separated from the tree, they keep their northwoods aroma. A good load of balsam would be ideal to set the Vermont scene for Piney down in Chincoteague.

I sawed the legs off the wooden cage and tried it on the back seat. It was lucky that the kids weren't coming; I don't know where we'd have put them. The cage took up most of the seat as it was. Removing the cage from the car, I put it on the porch with Piney so he'd get used to the smell of it over the next two days.

We put the boughs on the porch, too, so he'd become used to their fragrance. We hoped this would keep him from getting homesick at the carnival. The warmth of the summer day really brought out the scent in the still air of our front porch. It made us feel as if we were curing Piney like a ham in hickory smoke.

On Thursday night we packed everything but Piney and his playpen. We carefully stuffed those stiff balsam boughs into the trunk of the car. Our suitcases were ready but for the last-minute things which we would pack in the morning. With the coming of dawn we'd grab a hasty bite and load Piney and his teddy bear into his oversized travel case before he could protest.

Then, with any luck at all, we'd be at the first bookstore—complete with porcupine—just as the proprietor was opening for the day.

6

WE'D BEEN TRAVELING nearly two hours when we decided it was time for a rest stop. Piney, on the back seat, had been a good traveler so far. He'd taken his confinement philosophically, and was now crawling around the inside of the cage and hanging upside down from its woven-wire ceiling as if he enjoyed the motion of the car. Still, we thought he'd appreciate a change of scenery. He'd never been caged this long before. Therefore, when we spotted a gas station with a little grassy area, we stopped.

Pulling up to the gasoline pump, we got out of the car. The attendant, with the nonchalance born of long association with the stimulating world of undernourished gas tanks, put the hose in the filler pipe and turned it on. Then he looked over at me. "How many?" he asked.

"All it'll take," I answered, walking around in a little circle to get the kinks out of my legs.

Whistling idly, the attendant took the wet sponge and headed for the windshield. As he went by the back window, he glanced inside. Then he stopped, puzzled. Scowling against the glare of the morning sun, he peered closer. "Mind if I ask what kind of a cat that is?"

"Well," I joked, opening the door and lifting Piney out of his cage, "you might call him an angora. . . ."

The attendant recoiled. "Holy mackerel! A porcupine! Where'd you ever get a porcupine?"

So I told him Piney's story, while the hero of the tale nuzzled around in the grass. Then I strolled over to extract our pincushion pet from a little patch of clover he'd found.

As I lifted him there was a squeal of tires on the pavement. I glanced up to see a green sedan coming to a stop just past the entrance to the station. Every window was filled with curious faces. In a moment the car had backed up next to the other gasoline pump.

A man, with his wife and three children, got out. In a moment they were bearing down on us like hunters on safari. The man, fiddling with his camera, absently told the attendant to fill the tank.

"Watcha got there?" the woman asked, "a monkey?"

"No, ma'am."

"A raccoon?"

"Nope. I'll tell you what he is in a minute, but just for fun I'd like the kids to guess."

They jumped right into the game. They named every animal imaginable. Rabbit? Beaver? Skunk? Bear cub? Kangaroo? Mink? Weasel?

Finally, when the youngest ventured that maybe he was a penguin, I decided to let them in on the secret.

"Well, I'll tell you," I said, "his name's 'Piney.' Does that help you at all?"

"Oh, I know, I know!" squealed the toddler. "He's a pineapple!"

This convulsed the whole family. The lad was crestfallen, however, and I saw the tears in his eyes. So, when the laughter had quieted, I bent down to let him pet Piney. "That was a good guess," I said. "You got part of his name right. He's a porcupine."

The word meant little to him, but it had an immediate effect on the parents. "Yipes!" said the father, as he watched his youngest standing in the very jaws of death, "won't he throw his quills?"

For at least the twentieth time since we'd had Piney, I explained that he would never be so unfriendly. Then I told the wide-eyed youngsters and their camera-snapping father how we happened to have him along with us.

By now two other cars had stopped. Soon we had a little audience around us. It made me feel like one of those showmen with a potato peeler at a country fair. I told my listeners how old he was, where he lived, and what he ate. "He likes whole wheat bread," I concluded, "but he *loves* candy."

With this, the two older children turned and ran. In a moment they were back, breathless—each with a bar from the candy machine.

"Here's a Clark Bar for him!"

"No, let him have mine!"

Our contrary quill-pig, of course, chose not to receive either. "Actually," I said as I turned toward the car in answer to Peg's meaningful look at her watch, "most of the time he just has a plain chocolate bar."

Of course it was the wrong thing to say. The two raced back to the machine, this time accompanied by the youngest member of the family. Peg gave me a despairing glance, but it was too late to stop them. I waited while they made change and jiggled the knobs. Then they were back again.

This time Piney took the girl's chocolate bar and dutifully gave it a couple of nips. He bit a good chunk from the bar offered him by the youngest as well. Then, thank heaven, he put a few toothmarks in the older boy's chocolate, too. Having had four children myself, I was relieved that he'd treated them all alike.

Finally, to the accompaniment of clicking shutters, we managed to spirit Piney back into the cage.

With all those cameras, it reminded me of a press conference.

We started the engine just as the attendant was wiping the last windshield. "Sorry for the traffic jam," I said. "Hope it didn't louse things up for you."

"Hell, no," was the cheerful reply. "Drop in anytime. I sold more gas and candy and soda pop in ten minutes than I've sold in the last hour!"

Maybe George Sladen was right, at that. If this was the reaction of people who had never seen a porky before, perhaps he'd be worth the trouble, after all.

But of course there was the other side. There always is. The lady at the first bookstore where we stopped was happy to see us and make Piney's acquaintance. She quickly arranged a nook where, it was hoped, eager customers would throng to meet him and perhaps browse through her shelves on the way out.

Everything worked fine for a while. People came and met "Peg, Ron, and Piney Rood," as the hastily lettered sign proclaimed. A few, going past the window on their coffee break, ran and brought back a friend from the office. And each time we collected a little group, we'd tell about the pet that sat on my shoulder. After a time I almost began to wish porcupines *could* throw their quills, just so I wouldn't have to do so much explaining.

Suddenly, during one of my little talks, I felt Piney move. I looked up at him. Clutched in his paws was a rose—a blood-red, long-stemmed beauty. I glanced at the bookcase where I'd last seen the flower poised in a graceful, green-and-gold bud vase. Apparently I'd leaned against the shelf and Piney had taken the opportunity to gather the rose. The delicate vase was now teetering on the edge of the bookcase, and before I could make a move it had crashed to the floor. The vase contained a little water; it splashed with perfect accuracy over the top edges of the books standing on the bottom shelf. A wave of shocked silence spread over the store.

"Gosh," I said, as I helped the salesgirl remove the books, "I'm sorry."

Fortunately, the proprietor of the shop was a merciful soul. "Oh, *those* books," she said. "Think nothing of them. They're all going on sale next month, anyway. That's why they're on the bottom shelf." It was a gallant lie.

Still embarrassed by our pet's misbehavior I plucked him from my shoulder and held him at arm's length. He blinked at me with the rose between his teeth, like Carmen. "Piney, you rascal," I said, "you ought to be punished."

"That's right," someone volunteered. "Why don't you spank him?"

The comment tickled the onlookers, and the awkward moment passed. A few of the members of our little audience started coming forward to buy some of the water-damaged books. Peg and I, who are always eager for reading material, followed suit. Then, having helped the owner recoup a bit of her loss, we exited as gracefully as possible, complete with books, porcupine—and, of course, the rose.

Piney continued to attract attention at our other stops but, thank heavens, there were no further mishaps. We found a sympathetic motel owner that night who let us put the cage with its publicity-seeking occupant in an empty garage. We gave Piney his evening bottle under the interested eye of the owner and his family. Then we put him to bed.

It was the first night he'd been cramped up and all alone. He lost no time telling us about it, either. He began with a noise that sounded almost like the barking of a dog. Then he began to yodel. When this got no response, he switched to a whinny. Peg and I looked at each other. We could just imagine how Piney sounded to the other occupants of the motel.

I was all for going out to quiet him, but Peg wouldn't hear of it. "It's just like kindergarten on the first day," she said. "If I can only get Momma out of the room, little Cuthbert will scream for a while, and then he'll stop. If she comes back, he'll stop, too. But then he'll yell louder than ever when she goes away again."

So she made me sit it out. I knew that porcupines were accomplished vocalists, but up to now you couldn't have proved it by Piney. Now he made up for lost time. While Peg and I tried to read the books we'd bought at the store that morning, Piney went through his entire repertoire, with variations. The sounds ranged from a howl to a yowl, from a yip to a bark, and from a sneeze to a whimper.

Finally, however, he quieted down. Perhaps this would be the end of it for the night; he had been going at it for two hours. After one or two more outbursts to remind us of the foul deed we were perpetrating, he subsided.

In the morning we fed him, gave him his exercise, and put him in the car. As we stopped at the motel office to return the key, we met the people who had been in the unit next to ours. Hesitantly, I asked them whether the "puppy" had disturbed their slumbers.

"Naw," said the man. "As long as you know it's not yours, it doesn't bother you at all."

His reaction consoled us. Perhaps our stay in Chincoteague would be bearable, after all. At the Marina Motel, we'd made reservations for the end unit. Beyond it were a hundred feet of grassland, then the waters of Chincoteague Bay. This meant that if Piney got too impossible, we could put him out in the meadow and let him howl at the moon.

During the long, hot drive down the Delmarva Peninsula, we looked forward to an air-conditioned room. But it took us nearly an hour to make the last three miles. The sights—and smells—of the marshland captivated us. With the late afternoon sun at our backs, we were treated to the vision of myriads of birds. American and snowy egrets, in immaculate white plumage, glowed pink as their feathers caught the setting sun. Willets and sandpipers, wheeling in the crimson sky, seemed to burst into flame for a moment before settling down to earth.

Magenta-tinted great blue herons stood in the water, their deadly lances poised for unwary fish or crabs. One struck twice, quickly. Then, lifting that long stiletto of a beak, he shook a shower of sparks as he tossed a fiery tidbit down his skinny throat. Around him, sandpipers jabbed into the mud again and again, their slender beaks working like sewing machines as they probed for the marine worms and crustaceans uncovered by the retreating water.

Ducks, geese, brant, and coots flew squawking overhead or paddled in the shallows. Black skimmers, their blood-red bills made even more vivid by the flaming sun, glided swiftly just above the surface of the water. Now and again they dropped the lower mandible to scoop up the aquatic creatures that were unlucky enough to be floating in the topmost layer of water.

It was a fantasia of form and color and sound. The smell of tidal mud, so obnoxious to those who don't glory in the world of nature, was for us an aroma of richness and fertility. Basic to the living kaleidoscope around us, it is becoming more and more rare as man in his monstrous folly tries to fill in the precious marshlands.

We stopped, started, and stopped again and again along the causeway between the marshes. Other drivers impatiently pulled out and drove around us. I made a mental note to pick up one of the signs I'd seen on the back of a car at an Audubon Camp: "Birdwatcher—look out for sudden stops."

Finally our small passenger in the back seat reminded us that it was well beyond his suppertime. So, setting aside our binoculars and camera, we went on our way, arriving in Chincoteague at last with perhaps the first porcupine to occupy Virginia tidal soil in civilized history.

Steve Greene had sent his emissary, Andy Burrows, ahead to help prepare the way. With his trunk full of books and his head full of ideas, Andy had located the booth we were to occupy, and was ready with a sketch of how things might be situated. As he helped us unload the car, he suddenly stopped. "Gosh, Ron," he said, sniffing deeply, "what'd you folks bring with you, anyway? It even *smells* like Vermont."

Peg fitted the key to the trunk. "Fifty pounds," she said as she raised the lid, "of crisp mountain greenery."

She stood back to let Andy breathe in the aroma. It was as if we were standing in a balsam forest on the slope of Mount Mansfield. But there the similarity ceased.

We stared at the branches in surprise. The hardy

balsam, able to stand erect through the glittering cold of a sub-zero night, had wilted. In fact, after two days closed up in the hot trunk of the car it looked as if it had been cooked.

Peg picked out a piece and held it up. I'd seen stiffer branches on a weeping willow. "Well," my wife said as we viewed the remains, "there goes our atmosphere."

Andy, however, was more optimistic. There just had to be a spark of life there somewhere, he figured. So we hauled the discouraged branches into the motel room. Placing them in the tub, we closed the drain and turned on the cold shower.

After we'd soaked them, we propped them up in the water. Both of us had been looking forward to a shower, but we'd have to wait, even if it was Saturday night. Perhaps later, when they had drained off a little, we could set a few of the more promising ones in pans of water. Or at least we could take them out of the tub long enough for our own shower. I skinned the bark at the base of each branch with a knife. This was an old Christmas-tree trick; it allowed the trunk to take up water as fast as possible, and helped the tree retain its needles longer.

The Marina Motel is owned by the Leonards. Don Leonard was busy setting up the carnival, the sounds of which we could hear down the street. But his wife, having been warned about Piney, came to see him for herself as soon as we'd unloaded the car.

"I'll keep him outside," I promised. "He'll be in his cage, so he won't get into anything." I neglected to tell her about the midnight serenade.

But she wouldn't hear of it. "Why, the mosquitoes'll eat him alive. Besides, it's air-conditioned in here. He'd probably roast outdoors."

It *was* about twenty degrees cooler inside, at that. So we brought him in and fed him. Then, leaving him with his teddy bear, his air-conditioning, and a chunk of chocolate, we wandered down to visit the carnival.

A girl at a microphone was belting out a song about being in love with three boys at once. We each bought one of those wonderful oyster sandwiches and strolled over to listen to her.

At the far end of the grounds the Ferris wheel creaked out its tuneless rhythm. We wondered how a denizen of the quiet forests would react to all the ruckus—the staccato of the fortune wheels, the clatter of the tot-sized roller coaster, the singsong of the barkers, the twang of amplified guitars, the smell of cotton candy, hot popcorn, clam cakes, and oyster sandwiches.

After a look at the booth where we'd be setting up on Monday following the Sunday lull, we headed back for the motel. As we drew closer, we listened apprehensively. There was not a sound.

We quietly opened the door and took a peek at Piney. He was amusing himself by climbing around in his cage and scarcely seemed to hear the soft click of the latch. The noise of the air-conditioning probably drowned out the sound of our entrance. It had been running continuously since we'd arrived three hours before, and the place was like an icebox. So Peg turned it down for the night.

The minute the blower ceased, Piney began. Sensing our presence in the room, he started calling to us. So I turned the blower back on and he stopped again.

We'd just learned something about porcupine psychology. He was no different from dogs, or cats, or monkeys—or people, for that matter. My veterinarian friend, Don Gill, had put a radio in the animal room in back of his office. "It works like a charm," he told me. "The dogs used to be in an uproar when there was nobody in the room with them. But now the radio keeps them quiet."

I'd heard of orphan monkeys who pined for their mothers—until they were lulled by a ticking alarm clock. A baby often likes a clock, too—or a rattle or, of course, Mother's lullaby. And, as grownups, we still like to have our background music—even in office elevators.

Well, we'd have an air-conditioned sleep tonight. Vermont has a reputation for having two seasons— winter and tough sledding. Nevertheless, having mountain air blowing at us out of a wind tunnel did not make us feel at home.

Our porcupine apparently satisfied, we went in to look at his balsam boughs. One or two of them, happily, showed signs of awakening, so perhaps the air-conditioning would do the trick. We removed them from the bathtub, took quick showers, replaced them, and tumbled into bed.

Down the street I could hear the carnival still going on. Gradually, the sounds turned into a giant rushing waterfall. And into the woods near the cataract came a bulldozer, its machinery grating—crunch, crunch, crunch.

Then Peg jabbed me. "Go tell Piney to stop."

The waterfall and the bulldozer disappeared. I was back in the motel room. The rushing water was the blower of the air-conditioner. And the bulldozer was Piney, sharpening his teeth on the wooden post of his cage.

Of course there was no way to make him stop. Rodents have to gnaw to keep their teeth in shape. So I shut the door and left him in the living room with his air-conditioner. When our room began to get stuffy, we opened the window, but the air felt like a blast from a furnace after the coolness of the air-conditioner, so we gave up and opened the door to the living room again.

The last thing I remember was the welcome coolness—and that nibbler's nocturne coming through loud and clear.

7

OUR SPOT at the carnival was at one end of the large information booth. It was the nerve center of the entire show. We couldn't have asked for a better place.

When Junior got lost, some kind soul would bring him to the booth. There he'd stay, tear-stained and damp, until his lucky parents claimed him. Wandering parcels and abandoned pocketbooks were held there as well, until their owners discovered their loss. The microphone for the public address system was there, too, plus the branch facilities of Radio WDMV at Pocomoke City.

When it came time to set up the booth on Monday, we hauled the balsam out of the bathtub. I held the branches up for Peg's inspection. There were three boughs that were passable, but Peg said the rest of them looked like a bunch of dead chickens.

Still, they were all we had. Peg and Andy tacked them up on the wall but they looked more like palms than firs. So we decided to hang them upside down. That way their droopiness wouldn't be so obvious. At least they were approximately the right color, and the odor was there. Perhaps nobody would notice them.

We might end up talking to ourselves anyway, Peg decided. People came to the carnival to look at ponies and ride on merry-go-rounds, not to stand around and contemplate porcupines from Vermont. Piney might have been an attraction on the front porch or at a gas station, but here among the hurly-burly, things could be different.

Our scenery arranged, we went back to the motel for Piney. It was a hot afternoon, so we had been grateful for the cool room for Piney's sake. Accustomed to sleeping during the day, he was next to his teddy bear, eyes closed in slumber.

"Well," said Peg dramatically, as she reached into the cage, "this is it."

She held her hands open and Piney obligingly climbed onto her palms, placing each foot deliberately, as always: one—two—three—four. Then, while he blinked at the bright light, she took him out into the afternoon sun. "That's enough sleep for now, Piney. Time to go to work."

And so he did, with a vengeance. If I hadn't been

sure that such an idea could never enter his peaceful little head, I'd have sworn that this was just the chance he'd been waiting for.

Carl Briggs was first. Carl was the radio announcer on duty at the information booth when we arrived with Piney. Things hadn't really started yet, and Carl had probably been having a hard time keeping listeners entertained.

He seized on Piney at once. Figuratively, of course. He'd never met a porcupine before—certainly not at close range. So, while I held Piney, Carl described his small guest for his Delmarva Peninsula audience. With Piney on his shoulder, he said he felt like a sea captain with a prickly parrot. He described the softness of a porcupine's underside as contrasted to his brambly back and tail.

It was wonderful publicity. We'd have people flocking to us in no time.

Except for one thing. We weren't going out over the air. Piney, bless his heart, had already seen to that.

We discovered this fascinating fact when a boy came running across the fairgrounds. "Check your mike," he called. "Quick. They're on the phone at the station and say you're not coming through."

So Carl checked. Sure enough, we'd been talking to ourselves, just as Peg had predicted. While we'd been moving Piney from one shoulder to another and transferring the portable microphone in the close quarters of the booth, our hero had managed to get a black paw on the switch.

All that conversation for nothing. And by now most of the allotted time had run out. So, with a quick explanation of what had gone wrong, and with a promise to let his audience meet "Peg and Ron Rood and their electric porcupine" as soon as possible, Carl returned his listeners to the studio.

A small crowd had begun to collect in front of our booth, and when we finally finished the interview a dozen people pressed forward. Piney was on stage—as he would be for an almost unbroken two-week stand.

The reaction of those first few people was fairly typical. First they'd come to the counter of the booth, which, for an adult, was about breast-high. Often parents would lift their children so they could see. Then—in what seemed to us colossal trust, before they even knew what kind of animal he was—they'd reach out a hand and stroke Piney.

His standard reaction was to stretch out two hands to them. After all, porcupines are practically obsessed with the urge to grasp and climb anything within reach. This, of course, surprised them, and they'd hastily draw back.

Only then would they inquire about what kind of animal it was. When we told them, the trust returned. And, of course, the inevitable question. "But doesn't he throw his quills?" they'd ask, even as they ran a hand over his coat again, "or have you had him de-quilled?"

In answer, one of us would carefully rub his fur the wrong way and show them the hundreds of murderous spikes. We'd explain that he kept them sheathed beneath the outer guard hairs because, as one youngster remarked, "he thinks we're porcupines, too."

Impressed by our brisk business, Andy decided to keep track of how many people paid a visit to our tiny section of Vermont. It was a good idea that first night, when visitors were relatively few. The pony swim wouldn't be for another nine days, so the big wave of tourists hadn't hit town. Even at that, we were surprised at the end of the evening to find that exactly one hundred and fifty had come to see Piney.

We started to keep track again the second night, but after the first ten minutes we had to give up. People who had seen our porcupine the first evening went home and told others; the next night they were back with their acquaintances.

It was heartwarming to see them return. They treated Piney like an old friend. "I brought my brother with me," they'd say, half addressing us and half addressing the spiny creature, who reached out to their hands obligingly. Sometimes they'd introduce him as if he were a real human being: "Piney, this is Bill."

The children took him—almost literally—to

their hearts. We had to be constantly on the alert to prevent them from lifting him right off the counter and holding him like a puppy. The first evening we allowed it, but the next night we began to fear that he'd be petted to death. Even with those quills, he might get squeezed if some overamorous child grabbed him the wrong way.

With that constant petting, we saw there was another problem. A porcupine doesn't have a grumpy bone in its body, and Piney was no exception. He endured the slow caress, the firm stroke, the gentle pat, the rough touch with complete equanimity. But it was his nature to sleep during the day and we could see by the second afternoon that all this handling was getting to him.

Like a child who's too tired to slow down, he became more and more high-strung. He whirled around on the counter snatching at anyone who tried to pet him, in his eagerness to climb. I was afraid someone was going to get a scare, even if nobody really got hurt. Besides, when he wasn't trotting around on the counter he was climbing on us. It was a bit wearing.

So we figured he should have some means to escape from the endearments of his public. We should have some means to escape from him, too. But how?

Finally we got him a little stool. Porcupines, with their marvelous sense of balance and grasping feet and claws, are among the most surefooted of beasts. But they take no risks as far as climbing is concerned.

If they cannot tell with complete certainty where the next step will take them, they won't go. When we put Piney on his stool, therefore, he was as good as in a cage. With the rim of the stool projecting out beyond the legs, he couldn't quite negotiate himself out and over the edge. So he stayed on top, in full view, but on an island of his own.

This was fine—until the accident. It happened on the third day, and it almost put a stop to our whole show. A man stepped up to the counter. He had a tiny tot in his arms. "Is it all right if my son pets your porcupine?"

"Sure," I said, pleased that someone knew what kind of animal it was without being told.

The boy reached out as his dad leaned forward. At that moment, Piney turned in such a way that his tail stuck out toward the small hand.

"Oh, no!" said the father hastily, "not the tail!"

He stepped back impulsively. But it was too late. Those five baby fingers closed around Piney's nether appendage just as the lad's father jerked him away. Piney came off the stool and landed on the ground with a sickening thud.

Peg had been standing beside me. With the swiftness born of long practice in scooping up children who've fallen downstairs or had their fingers slammed in doors, she was out of the booth and around in front before I'd realized what had happened. But even at that, she was far slower than the man. To the surprise of both of us, he grabbed Piney by the scruff of the neck—somehow escaping even a single quill—and deposited him back on the stool.

Seldom have I seen a more contrite gentleman. And there was plenty of reason for his concern. Piney was as limp as death. Even the tot sensed that something was wrong, and remained unmoving in his father's arms.

Then, slowly, Piney pulled himself into a little ball. That was a relief; at least he was conscious. But he remained huddled up for several minutes while the stricken father did his penance. I felt sorry for the man and assured him it would take a lot more than that to damage a porcupine. I just hoped I was right.

Finally, after an eternity for all of us, Piney came to life. He stretched, stood up as tall as he could—and shook himself. The action was so unexpected that a laugh went up from the crowd. The crisis was over.

The man relaxed. "I just hope he's going to be all right," he said fervently. Then he was gone before anything further could happen. Perhaps he'll read these words; if so, he may be happy to know that Piney did, indeed, shrug it off completely. After all, even a surefooted porcupine must fall sometime. And they *are* tough; a few moments of holding a porcupine impresses you with the fact that he's built like a wrestler.

Even if he is almost invulnerable, however, there is one point where a porcupine is tender. That is his nose. A single blow to the nose, I'm told, will lay a porky low forever. This is probably why, in defense posture, his nose is hidden well down against his front paws. And it was Piney's nose that sparked his only display of temper. With all the mauling and manhandling during those two weeks, he lost his patience just once.

It was at the end of the first week. The crowds had been thick all afternoon, the day had been hot, but Piney had borne it well. Then a woman came up to the booth—one of those females who runs her husband, wears very practical shoes, and has all the answers.

"What's his name?" was her opening gambit.

"Piney-the-porcupine," I said, rattling it off for perhaps the two hundredth time that day.

"H-m-m-m. Porcupine. Aren't you afraid of him?"

"No, of course not. He wouldn't hurt a flea."

"Never?"

"Well, he hasn't hurt anybody yet—" This should have sufficed. But she was made of sterner stuff.

"I don't believe it," she interrupted, stroking him hard and rapidly, from nose to tail.

Piney usually grunted gently while he was being petted. Now those grunts increased in volume. "See?" her look seemed to say as she pressed down on him ever harder. "You don't know much about porcupines, do you?"

I felt sure she'd stop now. But, incredibly, she went on. Bending down, she looked Piney right in the eyes. Still rubbing him, she blew in his face. "Cut it out!" I yelped. But my outburst was too late. Piney retaliated—instantly and completely.

With a slap, his tail jerked upward. Every quill stood on end. He looked twice the size he'd been a moment before—all white-spiked and dangerous.

The woman jumped backward. She stared at her wrist. There were ten or a dozen quills embedded in the flesh, plus a few in the strap of her wrist watch.

Her mouth opened. Then it shut again. Finally she found her voice. "What that porcupine needs," she declared, shaking her finger as close to him as she dared, "is a good spanking!" Then, wonderingly: "But how do you spank a porcupine?"

I offered to help her, but she disdained my assistance. She'd been met and bested in fair combat, and was honest enough to admit it. Stalking off, she disappeared into the crowd.

A small boy had watched the entire proceedings. "Gee!" he said as he gingerly reached out to pet the now subdued Piney, "that's some porcupine! How much do you want for him?"

I smiled. "Piney? He's not for sale."

"But how much would you want for him if he *was* for sale?"

I'd never thought of Piney as having any price. But I told him that if pet stores sold porcupines, they'd probably go for about twenty dollars.

He was a persistent chap.

"I'll give you twenty-five."

"Nope. I told you—he's not for sale."

He shrugged and went away. But he returned within the hour.

"Thirty?"

"I told you already, son. I'm not selling him."

"Okay." Cheerfully, he went away again.

He came back again a couple of nights later, this time with two of his cronies. "Thirty-five?"

I smiled and shook my head.

"Forty?"

"No."

They went into a huddle. Then the small entrepreneur stood and faced me squarely. "I— We'll give you forty-two fifty," he announced. "And that's my tops."

I hated to disappoint this budding Barnum, but I was glad he'd named his top figure. It was embarrassing to have somebody offering common money for your own flesh and blood, so to speak. So I refused his last generous offer with relief, breaking the news as gently as I could. Of course it didn't faze him a bit.

"That's all right," he assured me, "there'll be other porcupines."

And I'm sure there will be, too—for him, at least. In fact, the very next night he showed up with a box turtle. "Got it from a boy for a goldfish and two paper clips," he announced. "You ain't changed your mind about the porcupine?"

When I shook my head, he closed the door on my golden opportunity forever. "That's all right," he said, "neither have I."

His was the highest bid. However, we did have a number of other offers. In fact, when Peg sent a note to Andy Burrows, who had gone back to Vermont after setting us up at the carnival, she told him of the offers we'd had for our pet.

"Send us a hundred porcupines," she concluded. "We'll clean up."

Actually I doubt if Piney would have survived very long in Virginia. The heat of their summer was almost more than he could bear. Whenever he got a chance he'd lie down, feet stretched out front and rear, puffing rapidly as if he'd been running a race. He seemed to be able to sweat very little, if at all, so he had no way to combat the heat. We were grateful for our air-conditioned room; on one afternoon when the heat was fierce, I took him back and left him there, even though the carnival was in full swing.

One day when Piney was suffering excessively from the heat, Carl Briggs brought him a big paper cup filled with ice and water. A porcupine doesn't lap water like a dog but swallows it in long draughts, the way a human would do if he lay on his stomach to drink from a brook.

Piney gratefully buried his snout in the cold water. When Carl decided he'd had enough, he set the cup out of reach. But Piney continued to grope toward it, so Carl fished out a couple of big chunks of ice for him to chew. Perched on his stool, he nibbled them before a delighted audience of onlookers. Then he paused. Appearing to consider for a moment, he dropped the ice on the stool. Then he calmly lay down on top of it and went to sleep.

Peg put the paper cup under one edge of the stool to catch the drip. And there Piney stayed until the last bit of ice had melted.

People were surprisingly considerate of Piney if we explained his porcupine ways. So when Piney was sleeping, Peg and I would often hold a finger up to our lips, and speak in a low tone.

We've discovered that a whisper is more disturbing to a wild animal than a low, quiet voice. A visitor, once he understood, would reply in kind—and Piney would slumber on undisturbed.

Frequently, people asked if Piney could do tricks. Not content with observing a live porky, they wanted a waltzing bear as well. When we explained that, to us, a wild animal trained to do tricks was ridiculous and pathetic, they'd shake their heads. "You see them all the time on television," was the rejoinder. Apparently this made it all right.

Nor did we try to train him in personal hygiene. This would have imposed human standards where they didn't belong. Our visitors often inquired as to whether he was housebroken. While Piney had his own corner of the front porch which we kept covered with newspapers, we had to confess that he wasn't very fastidious. Porcupines never are. After all, they spend as much as two weeks, sometimes, in a single tree, and when you're up in the air like that, sanitation is no problem at all.

Since the fecal pellets are actually dry little sausage-shaped objects a little larger than jelly beans, they are no problem in the woods. To try to turn a porky into a non-porky by housebreaking him wouldn't be right. It would be just as pointless as teaching him to ride a bicycle—which I'm sure a porcupine, with his sense of balance, could readily do.

Besides that oft-repeated "does he throw his quills?" there were a number of other standard questions. Second in popularity was "does he bite?" followed closely by "when does he get his quills?" to which we'd reply by stroking Piney against the grain to show that he already had them.

Then people wondered why he didn't get stuck with his own quills. Of course, the barbed ends of the quills were always pointed away from him. And even if one of them did become lodged, it would probably turn and lie harmlessly beneath the outer skin, which slides readily back and forth over his compact, muscular body.

A number of people assumed that Piney had been de-quilled, something in the manner of an expurgated skunk, I suppose. On rare occasions when someone was really interested, I'd ask him for a handkerchief or other item of clothing, press it firmly up into the tips of Piney's hidden quills, and then yank it away. Usually one or two quills, caught in the cloth by their barbs, would come free. This never ceased to amaze Piney's rapt audience. The person would go away, carefully folding the handkerchief, having acquired a fascinating souvenir.

But of course not everyone was delighted by Piney. Peg jotted down an entire conversation between a mother and her small son:

"What is it, Peter?"

"A porcupine, the man says."

"A porcupine! Ugh! Come away!"

And with that, she pulled him off to other, safer interests.

Then there was the little girl who lost her balloon when Piney tried to embrace it. And Piney managed to wrest some cotton candy from another girl who was petting him with the cone in her hand.

And we all got in the act when Piney managed to get a two-handed grip on the hair curlers of a sweet young thing. Most of the time we could rectify such mishaps with a quick apology—plus a new balloon, a second helping of fuzzy candy, or whatever the occasion demanded.

There was one place where I felt Piney could get in no trouble at all; that was the lawn in front of our motel. But one evening after work he proved me wrong.

While I idly sat and watched, our little vegetarian placidly mowed his way through a tiny patch of four-leaf clovers. The patch had been discovered by a small motel guest that afternoon and the clover was being left to grow until the boy was ready to go home. He'd even checked with the management to be sure they would not cut the lawn by mistake. But he'd forgotten to check with Piney.

Fortunately, I was able to swap a few quills for the unlucky clovers. Except for these little surprises, however, our small Vermonter managed to make friends wherever he went. In fact, when it came time to give one of my lectures, a listener joked: "You don't have to bother to say anything. Just show us the porcupine."

When we totaled up the number of visitors on the last day, it was quite an impressive figure: during Chincoteague's two-week carnival, an estimated ten thousand people had passed by our little section of the information booth. Piney seemed to thrive through it all, and was as eager to make new friends on the last day as he had been on the first.

Our porcupine had proved to be an overall asset.

He'd even helped us sell a few books. But, as we packed our things and prepared to return, there was one question that remained: recalling the lady who'd collected the quills in her arm, the girl with her hair curlers askew, the dead microphone, and the unlucky four-leaf clovers, I asked myself, just how *do* you spank a porcupine?

8

WHEN WE GOT BACK to Vermont, there was a letter waiting. It was from a schoolteacher friend.

"We're making plans for the fall term," Mrs. White wrote. "Could you bring your porcupine for the children to see?"

At that moment we'd had enough. The jaunt to Chincoteague had been fun, but it had been tiring, too. I wanted to put Piney back on the porch. Then little by little, I planned to allow him the run of the yard. Hopefully this would be the beginning of his return to the wild.

At least that was the original plan, but Piney hadn't read the schedule. He had been weaned; we finished the milk-and-honey routine while we were still in Virginia, but his experience in Chincoteague had spoiled him. Now that he was a box-office smash, we wondered if he'd ever forsake the limelight. It would take a lot of undoing to erase from his memory the sound of voices, the feel of human hands, and the noisy excitement of the carnival. It had certainly not been a satisfactory dress rehearsal for the solitude of a Vermont forest.

One day as we watched the evident good nature with which Piney accepted the attentions of his human friends Peg said, "I don't know how you think you'll ever make a wild porcupine out of him again."

Obviously the way things were at the moment, he was about as ready for our woodlands as a Mexican Chihuahua. To him the sound and scent of a human meant food, shelter, a pat on the head. Yet, to survive in the forest he'd have to protect himself from man.

This is how it was when the letter arrived. Mrs. White's request hit me in a vulnerable spot. As one who has been a teacher most of his adult life, I could see that Piney would be a perfect audiovisual aid, particularly in Vermont where feelings against porcupines ran high. Given this opportunity I could hope to persuade the school children that there is, indeed, a place for everything. It was worth a try.

"Besides," Peg pointed out, obviously relishing her play on words, "we're stuck with the porcupine, anyway. Why not make the best of him?"

I winced at the idea of exploiting Piney. It was against everything I'd tried to tell my own students. How could I preach against the taking of wild animals as pets with a porcupine on my shoulder? But if this was to be a double standard we'd make the most of it.

I told Mrs. White I'd accept her invitation. Then Peg and I followed up by writing to a number of fellow teachers whose requests for porcupine talks we had previously refused. "And as long as we're about it," Peg said licking the envelope, "we might as well see what other teachers would like to meet Piney."

Now that we had decided to keep him for a while, the star of our show had to have quarters befitting his exalted position. I built a little platform in a top corner of the porch and tacked cleats on the wall leading to it so that he could reach it from two directions. Fletcher and Hattie Brown brought a jeepload of wood for the fireplace which we stored on the porch with the hope that Piney would prefer it to the woodwork. And Peg, who had been after me to paint the porch, sighed and said it might as well wait a little longer.

During the summer, our porcupine could use the platform for his day-long snooze. But with the coming of cold weather he might be grateful for more protection, so I created a den out of an old packing box lined with straw. If we still had him during the winter I'd cover it with a couple of old sleeping bags. Then, looking still further ahead to next spring, I would make him an outdoor cage.

Piney's presence as a welcoming committee was

not always an unmixed blessing. A friend, who burst into our kitchen one day without knocking, looked back through the window at a disappointed porcupine and asked sheepishly, "How do *I* know he's friendly?"

Then there was the afternoon when Bob and Pat Armstrong arrived for a picnic with a bag full of fresh-picked Bibb lettuce, sent to us by Pat's parents. They didn't see Piney, who was slumbering on his platform in the corner of the porch. Thinking the lettuce would be cooler there, they left it on top of his den. And, as it was to be a surprise, they carefully refrained from telling us about it.

It wasn't long, I imagine, before that square black nose began to twitch. Guided by his unerring sense of smell, Piney stirred from his reverie, backed down his ladder, and waddled across the floor. He then nuzzled his way into the bag and proceeded to create his own version of a tossed salad.

Recalling the fate of the lady's umbrella handle a couple of months earlier, we realized people should be forewarned. So I rummaged around in our garage until I found a sign Roger had made a couple of years ago. BEWARE OF THE SQUIRREL, it said, referring jokingly to a playful gray who had the disconcerting habit of jumping up in your arms whether you invited him or not. I hung the sign on the front door of the porch, and changed the word squirrel to porcupine. As an afterthought, I added that he was harmless, but if visitors were doubtful they could use the other door.

Piney didn't spend all his time on the front porch, however. He was much too personable for that. Guests who came to call usually demanded to see him. This was fine with us because he was a perfect conversation piece. Either we'd bring him into the house, or, if the occasion was a picnic, we'd lodge him in the little apple tree next to the picnic table. Then, as we watched his antics, the guests would ask all those questions with which we'd become so familiar in Chincoteague.

There was one question, however, that the visitors at the carnival had not quite dared to ask. The people who came to our house apparently felt they knew us well enough to put it to us: with all those quills, what is the process of mating like for porcupines?

It was a question that had intrigued us as well. So keen are the ears and noses of porcupines that they've seldom been surprised during a tender moment in the wild. But pet porcupines aren't as bashful, and have yielded their secrets on a number of occasions. Piney, of course, couldn't help us out. He wouldn't reach his maturity for another year.

But some of the books we'd collected described the process. David F. Costello's fine work *The World of the Porcupine* (Lippincott, 1966) pointed out that mating may occur from September to December. The female has a regular cycle of heat. It is repeated approximately every thirty days, especially during the fall, so that if she doesn't find a mate one month, she may be luckier the next. This explained why I had seen mother porcupines with their young as early as April and as late as July.

Costello's book, based on years of experience and painstaking research, indicated that the female becomes nervous and jittery when she is in heat. During that period she deposits many little puddles of urine. She may also moan, chatter her teeth, and squeal.

Her swain, hearing—and scenting—her condition, responds with an unearthly serenade. And when he comes across a spot of her urine, he solemnly adds some of his own.

When the male and female get together, further gentle words are spoken. During this period the betrothed couple may stand erect, nose to nose with front paws touching. Benighted humans, encountering the porcupines at that point, have assumed that it was the moment of truth. To our way of thinking, it would make sense for mating to occur in this manner; in that way neither of the lovers would get any quills by mistake.

Actually, this is just the engagement. After such a rousing courtship, the marriage is almost an anticlimax. The unadorned truth, as Costello points out, is that the porcupines assume the same mating position as most other four-footed mammals.

After we'd satisfied the curiosity of our questioners on this score, there would be a moment of contemplation. Then, predictably, the next question would follow: all right, so love among the porcupines is no problem. But how about birth? How does the mother give birth without getting quilled in the process?

The fact is that little porkies are born encased in a sac, just like puppies, kittens, or calves. The quills of the newborn baby, though soft with moisture, are fully formed. As soon as the sac is broken, they begin to dry and are ready for action. Of course a youngster has nowhere near the thirty thousand quills estimated to be borne by his parent, but he has enough spines to defend himself, as Piney had so ably demonstrated. The mature female bears but a single young each year. She has four nipples, or mammae, and the nursing porkie alternates from one to another until his appetite is satisfied.

Again, Costello tells us that young porkies in captivity have been known to nurse for four months. This answered our question about Piney. He had, as we suspected, been near starvation when we found him.

Other questions regarding porcupine characteristics inevitably arose. Did his quills grow back after they had been shed? Of course; after all, they were really modified hairs. How long do porcupines live? It's hard to say, because all wild animals face hazards, but tame ones have been known to live ten years.

This response prompted one wit who noticed Piney lying motionless on his platform to ask, "Do you call that living?"

One day a letter arrived in the mail from the editor of a national magazine, asking me to do an article on my porcupine. Of course I wanted to do it. But it brought up the question of whether we could insure Piney. After all, he was turning into a valuable property.

I called our insurance agent, Stan Bryden. "Stan, I'm going to ask you something that'll make you laugh."

I didn't have to go any further. Stan was laughing already. "Not your porcupine!" he choked.

"Come on, Stan. Be serious. I've got to write a story about him. With pictures. I don't want anything to happen before I'm through. You know what would happen to him if he wandered away. The first person he met—blooey!"

Stan solemnly vowed that he'd try to help me. A week later he called me on the telephone. "I have a communication from the main office, Ron. Could you call your porcupine a domestic animal?"

"Well—he's tamed, if that's what you mean."

"But people don't regularly buy and sell porcupines the way they do cows and horses and pigs, Ron."

I had to admit it was true. But I reminded him that we'd bought a Chincoteague pony who'd been as wild as Piney when we first got him, "and you've got him insured." Stan still had his doubts, but said he'd try again.

Another week went by before Stan called. It wasn't going to work. The insurance company, with millions in resources, didn't want to go out on a limb, so to speak, with a porcupine. There just wasn't any established market value on porkies. They couldn't insure him if they didn't know what he was worth.

I cherish the correspondence:

"Gentlemen (the letter from the insurance company began): I have tried every avenue I know of but unfortunately each one ended in a dead end as far as the above captioned exposure is concerned."

It was dutifully signed by James L. Mulligan, Special Agent. And solemnly, in the space above the body of the letter, the secretary had typed: "Re: Porcupines."

Eleanor Adams, Stan's secretary, had appended a note of her own: "Ron: We are sorry but we do not have any outlets to obtain coverage on your porcupine."

Actually, we knew a porcupine must seem far removed from the main office with its fluorescent lights, its statistics, and its coffee breaks. But we knew, also, that if I'd appeared in the president's executive suite with Piney on my shoulder, I'd have had as interested an audience as I'd ever had in

Chincoteague. Piney *was* important—even if the company didn't think he was worth insuring.

So this became our next task—to instill an appreciation of porcupines in the minds of those who might read about him but never meet him. We had an obligation to the school children, too. One day they might hold his very life in their hands. How much they learned today would mean everything tomorrow.

The children, of course, were more than willing to meet him halfway. Mrs. White's class was my first. When I got to the school and parked in the front driveway, there was no question as to which was her room. The windows were full of faces. Twenty pairs of eyes followed my every move as I got out of the car, lifted the lid of Piney's cage, and put him on my shoulder. And when I got to the door of the room, I had no need to knock.

Those who deplore the mess into which our youth have fallen should take a good look at these youngsters while they're in the lower grades of school. They haven't been everywhere yet, nor have they seen everything. Their eyes are wide, their smiles spontaneous. They are skinny, fat, awkward, clumsy, angular, with feet too big and pants too short. Their comments are quick, penetrating:

"If a quill keeps going into you, does it come out the other side?" (Yes, occasionally. Sometimes it gets into a blood vessel and floats along until it gets stuck again.)

"My father says porcupines sleep right in their own manure." (That's right, son. Especially in the winter, when a number of them may "den up" under a shelving rock. You can hardly blame them, though, with two feet of snow outside. Actually their fecal pellets are fairly dry anyway. And as soon as the weather allows a porcupine to travel, he may head for the highest tree. There he'll stay—blizzards and all. He doesn't hibernate.)

"If they eat so much wood, why don't they get splinters?" (Porkies are as deliberate about chewing as about everything else. They chew their food into tiny bits so there are no splinters left.)

"Which would win a fight, a porcupine or a skunk?" (A porcupine, hands down. The scent is unpleasant but the quills are deadly. The only thing is, I doubt if they'd ever fight. They're both pacifists.)

The comments, the questions, the answers went on and on. Toward the end of the session, I'd let them do the thing they were all waiting for—pet a live porcupine.

I had been trying to find words to describe how a porcupine felt when you petted him—the combination of coarse guard hairs, the half-hidden tips of the spines, and the yielding warmth of an animal body.

But it remained for Janet Lynch, in the sixth grade of Burlington's Flynn school, to supply them to me.

"Oh!" she said in wonder, "he feels just like shredded coconut!"

This is just the way Piney does feel. Except that coconut isn't warm, and doesn't respond when you stroke it.

One day I was giving a talk before a fifth grade class when there was a telephone call for me. One of the students immediately volunteered to take charge of Piney while I was gone. "We had a pet porcupine once, Mr. Rood. I'll see that he's all right until you get back."

When I returned, he was all right, all right. But the room wasn't in such good condition. A geranium lay on the floor underneath the plant shelf surrounded by pieces of a clay pot.

There were several more overturned plants on the shelf. The class stood in a stunned knot behind the teacher, with the porcupine expert well to the rear. And Piney, soaking wet, was chewing on the handle of the pencil sharpener.

I hurried over to him and stretched out my palm for him to climb on. Grunting companionably, he placed four damp, cold feet on my hand and wrist. Then, while the class relaxed, the teacher told me what had happened.

It seems that the boy who'd had a porcupine suddenly remembered that his "porcupine" had, in reality, been a rabbit. The revelation struck him when the persistent quill-pig started hoisting himself up his arm and shoulder. The boy managed to scrape Piney off on a chair—which would have been fine but for one thing. The back of the chair was resting against a broad shelf, and on the shelf was the window garden.

Piney lost no time in climbing up the chair and onto the shelf. There, reveling in the greenery, he disported himself like a calf in clover before his fascinated audience.

He had taken a good nip out of the jade plant. He'd clambered over the side of the aquarium and nosed around for the water plants. Then, leaving the fish still darting around in a panic, he had sloshed across the geraniums to the pencil sharpener. And there I picked him up—just in time to see the little wooden knob of the sharpener drop in two pieces to the floor.

It had all been done in less than five minutes. Of course, once the porcupine got in the plants, nobody knew how to get him out. Actually there wasn't much damage, but I wouldn't have given a nickel for the superintendent's chances if he'd offered the teacher a renewal contract just then.

For all his deliberate ways, Piney's four-fingered hands were amazingly quick. They got him into another scrape—this time before an audience of hundreds of delighted onlookers. His bizarre appearance combined with manifest good nature made him a natural for television. One such show involved Piney and a second guest, a gentleman sportsman who was well known for always wearing dark glasses. The gentleman and I were seated close together on little stools. Piney, as usual, was on my shoulder. At one side was the announcer with a table covered with products which, doubtless, Piney and his human friends were supposed to endorse by their presence. The lights were bright and hot, and I wished I had a pair of dark glasses myself. Apparently Piney did, too—the pair that the gentleman was wearing.

I kept him away from temptation all through the show, but when the interview was finished, I almost collapsed. The man on the other stool relaxed, too, leaning toward me as he fumbled for a cigarette.

Piney, seeing his chance, made one deft swipe— and the glasses were his. And just at that instant the camera flashed back on us for a final shot. It must have been a wonderful tableau: Piney and me struggling with the glasses, while the guest star stood betrayed, like a Moslem woman shorn of her veil. I'm told we were terrific on television.

We were making guest appearances at least once a week; we sometimes made as many as two or three. We used the opportunity to introduce and discuss the porcupine and to talk about wildlife in general.

My experience has taught me that every animal has its own fascinating story, and I used Piney to help me press the point.

After all, what more unlikely animal could you choose to display before an audience? Almost any outdoor story that mentions a porcupine dismisses him as a waddling, dim-witted, uninteresting creature, who chews everything in sight and rattles his quills at all who dare to stand in his way.

We had to admit that part of the myth was true. Piney *did* waddle; he was hopelessly bandy-legged. His toes turned in so that he sometimes stepped on his own feet. And I suppose he would never have made it through the first page of an I. Q. test, either, even if his dimness was in good part due to those myopic raisin eyes.

He was certainly self-centered; to ignore him was about as easy as trying to stop a water hose with your thumb. But persistence is supposed to be a virtue. As someone has said: "When you do it, it's stubbornness. When I do it, it's persistence."

That well-known trait of gnawing through everything is related, of course, to the porcupine's desire for salt. Here in Vermont, salt is put on the roads in the winter to melt the snow. A friend of mine who left his jeep in the woods overnight returned to find that the salty tires had been nibbled. One was bitten clear through. It .was studded with quills, too—apparently in retaliation for the explosion.

Some people protect their property by sprinkling salt on a nearby stump. The rain soaks the salt down through the wood and the porkies chew it to bits. So the porcupines get their salt and the owner gets rid of a stump.

Yes, admittedly, much that's said about porkies is true. But as to the charge that they are uninteresting —those are fighting words to Piney's three thousand personal acquaintances. I have a tape made at a Chamber of Commerce banquet which records the howls of delight that went up when I gave Piney half a lemon. He sat there and consumed the whole thing without blinking an eye. The sour, sour juice dripped off his elbows while the audience roared with laughter and I got it all on tape.

Uninteresting? Not to *these* diners!

I've seen the results of a porky who gnawed his way right through the heavy lead shielding of a telephone cable—apparently delighting in the sound and taste of teeth against metal. On my shelf are eleven eyelets from a pair of hunting boots, spit out by a porcupine after he had cut the tough leather into bite-sized pieces. But I didn't really know about the teeth of a porcupine until Piney took a fold of the skin of my forearm between those orange-yellow knives. With infinite gentleness he held my flesh while he murmured a greeting to me in his own peculiar language.

Nor did I understand the porcupine's amazing control of his quills until I'd seen him comb his hair by the simple process of erecting every spine and letting it fall carefully in place again. And the dexterity and strength of those hands and feet were surprising. Unable to hug the porch woodwork as he would a tree limb, Piney slipped off the smooth surface more than once. Unperturbed, he'd hang by a single claw and pull himself back to safety without ruffling a quill.

We even found a practical use for our quill-pig. Monday mornings at our house aren't much different, probably, from those in other homes; things are slow in getting started. Roger, in his fifteen-year-old lethargy, is the slowest of all. But if you put a porcupine in bed with even the sleepiest boy, it's not long before he's up on his feet to escape that animated pincushion. Piney made a perfect alarm clock —you couldn't just shut him off. This was an alarm clock that came back for more.

Don Gill, my veterinarian friend, suggested still another use for him. "When you're having a fancy meal," Don said, "just stick a bunch of hors d'oeuvres on his quills. Then set him on the dinner table to walk around so everybody can pick what they want. He'd be better than a lazy susan."

It was an education both to watch him and to listen to the comments of those who made his acquaintance. And my education was furthered, too, when I took him out in the woods to see how much wildness might be left in him after six months. But he apparently knew a good thing when he had it: he paid no attention to the beckoning wilderness, but followed me around like a puppy.

So, as Peg had so aptly put it, we were, indeed, stuck with him—any way you wanted to figure it.

9

My brother Jim and his wife Arline arrived from Hawaii with their three children in late summer. He had never brought his entire family back East before, and the presence of a real northwoods porcupine put the children in a transport of joy.

Four-year-old Melanie loved to have Piney nuzzle through her hair, even though, as we discovered later, he was giving her a raggedy haircut on the side. Celeste, two years older, stood in openmouthed amazement as he obligingly accepted a square of bitter cooking chocolate and manfully ate the whole thing.

Luckily, Denise had been the one to bring the orchid. I doubt if the younger ones would have understood. The children had been so interested in Piney that we'd just let him run free in the downstairs rooms—followed closely by the three delighted youngsters. But even the attraction of an exotic porcupine fades, and Piney was forgotten.

When next we thought of him, it was too late. They found him placidly sitting in the middle of the kitchen table, the last shreds of Denise's magnificent Cattleya orchid clutched in his paws. He'd removed it from its vase and hardly spilled a drop.

I trundled him out to his porch in a fury, but of course there was nothing that could be done. Denise smiled bravely and decided he must have been hungry. Peg, to whom the orchid had been given, philosophically made the best of it. Who but our family, she asked, would bring a priceless bloom through quarantine, and transport it for six thousand miles just so a porcupine could have orchids for dinner?

Besides, there were more orchids up in our woods, anyway. Not the exotic beauties of the tropics, but orchids nevertheless. To ease Denise's heartbreak, we went on an expedition to find them.

They were growing along the nature trail where we'd found Piney several months before: the ribbed twin leaves of the moccasin flower or common lady's slipper (*Cypripedium*). The blooms were gone, but the leaves remained. Later I was able to show them some colored slides I'd taken of the pouch-shaped pink blossoms. We found the remaining leaves of the magenta-and-white showy lady's slipper, too—a lovely flower which I had also been lucky enough to capture on film.

Then, just to prove that there were also orchids in bloom, I took them along the trail beneath the hemlocks where I'd found and labeled a little congregation of rattlesnake plantain (*Epipactis*). The spikes of tiny creamy-white flowers stood erect over the basal rosette of dark, snake-patterned leaves. On the way back through the meadow above the house we found lady's tresses (*Spiranthes*), with their greenish-white spikes of little flowers poking up through the grass.

The children weren't at all sure that such tiny blossoms were orchids until I showed them under a magnifying glass. When magnified several times their normal size, the blooms took on a more familiar appearance. Now we could see a lower lip and the upper sepals, flung out to the side in a fashion that reminded them of the flowers of their own bountiful land. This, of course, is the key to relationship among plants—the flowers, which appear similar despite wide variety in size and vegetative parts.

Finally, after I'd satisfied my tutorial instincts, I allowed school to recess for the day. Piney's unexpected lunch hadn't been a complete loss, after all.

"No wonder Piney ate Aunt Peg's flower," one of the children confided, "look at the size of the little orchids he has to eat around here."

Now that they'd figured out a perfectly logical excuse for Piney's actions, he became their fast friend.

One day we put him on the kitchen stool to see how long it would take for him to find his way down. He sniffed over the edge, climbed up on the back, reached out in space. After each attempt, he clasped his hands together a moment, and reached out again. Then, backing as far over to the edge as he could, he felt around with his tail. He could touch the leg of the stool, but it was of smooth, tubular steel and didn't offer much hope of a foothold, so he'd climb back up on the seat again.

We watched him for ten minutes, and he didn't seem to be making a bit of progress. Hands, feet, and tail—all explored to no avail. Jim and Arline, not aware that Piney probably couldn't see the floor clearly enough to tell just how far away it was, decided that he was just plain slow.

Denise bristled at this aspersion upon her friend. "Well, it's not his fault!" she snapped. "If you had to think everything out with four feet and a tail, you'd be slow, too!"

Piney finally did figure out the combination to the stool. At long last he learned to back confidently over to the edge and slide down the leg of the stool like a fireman.

There was one individual, however, who failed to succumb to Piney's charm. That was our dog, Rebel.

He had never forgiven the quill-pig for what he'd done to him up on that trail.

In his day, Rebel had frolicked with raccoons, skunks, squirrels, muskrats, woodchucks, and assorted other creatures who shared our home for various lengths of time. And he'd often go out to the pasture to try to entice Little Fellow into chasing him. Sometimes Yankee, a seven-year-old thoroughbred who'd been given to us by his disgruntled owners after he'd all but fallen asleep at post time, would join in the race.

But toward Piney, our dog remained steadfastly aloof. If he got shut out on the front porch he'd scratch at the door to come in. If we pretended not to notice him, he'd go over in the corner, heave a big sigh, and lie down to try to make the best of it.

Piney, however, with his usual good grace, was willing to let bygones be bygones. If in his absent-minded wanderings he happened to scent Rebel, he'd waddle over to investigate. Rebel would wait until the last minute; then, just as Piney's nose came up against him, he'd spring to his feet and run to the other corner.

It looked like a game, but it wasn't. Perhaps we gave entirely too much attention to Piney. At any rate, in his doggy fashion, Rebel seemed to rue the day he'd first set eyes on that pesky porky. And his feelings on the matter were revealed in an unusual way.

We first noticed it when Piney was sitting on the kitchen stool one evening, eating peanuts. Sometimes we didn't bother shelling them; it was fun to watch him crunch through them, shucks and all. Rebel, hearing the crackling and smacking of Piney's lips, wandered over near the stool and began to sniff among the debris on the floor. When he found a fragment of peanut, he promptly ate it.

"Why, Rebel," said Peg in surprise, "I didn't know you liked peanuts."

It was news to me, too. He'd never touched peanuts before. We watched as he cleaned up every piece.

Then we understood—or at least we think we did. A few moments after Piney had finished his meal, he did his fireman act and slid down the chairleg to the floor. As usual, he sniffed around through the shells, but Rebel's nose was as good as his. There wasn't a crumb left. Our canny pup had eaten those peanuts just so Piney couldn't have them.

We hated to impugn the motives of our pooch, but when Rebel did the same thing with grapes—another food he'd never eaten before—we were sure we had guessed right. After all, any farmer knows that two pigs in one pen will often eat more than two pigs in two pens. They stuff themselves just to keep the other one from getting the food.

On one or two occasions, Rebel even ate bits of lettuce that dropped from Piney's table. However, after a couple of trials, he gave it up. Anything as distasteful as that, he seemed to say, was just what the porcupine deserved.

There was one "table," however, from which Piney would feed without Rebel showing the slightest interest. That was the big tree. It was one of four huge maples on our front lawn, and it had a low branch on which I often put our porcupine. We figured that such a large tree could stand the loss of a little greenery with no ill effects.

When I placed him on his limb, Piney would sniff after me for a moment and then proceed to search for twigs. Sometimes he'd climb out of sight. Then the only way I'd be able to tell where he was located was by the slow trickle of leaves and shreds of bark from his section of the tree.

Those keen ears were ever alert, however. If I wanted him, I'd just have to go to the base of the tree and speak quietly: "Piney."

The scattering of debris would stop momentarily. Then it would triple in volume as Piney obediently came down the tree in reverse, loosening bark and twigs in the process. Soon he'd appear, that ever-probing tail feeling the way until he reached my upraised hand. Then, grunting his hunh-hunh-hunh, he'd shinny down my arm. When that lethal tail came to my face, he'd feel around carefully until he found just the right position. Then he'd turn, settle on my shoulder, and murmur important things into my ear.

When he was up in his tree about twenty feet he'd be opposite the window of my upstairs study. I could glance out and keep an eye on him as I typed or read a book. I watched as he gathered in a bunch of leaves, sometimes with one hand, sometimes with two, and ate them in bites, the way we'd eat the wrong end of a stalk of celery. At other times, he'd nibble the bark off a twig, or a fair-sized limb.

Often he'd hang on to a different twig with each foot, reminding me of the old cartoon of the man with one foot on the dock and the other on the row-boat. But precarious footing never bothered Piney; if a twig proved too supple, he still had a firm grip with his other appendages. So confident was he that he would sometimes gather a whole armload of twigs and back himself right out to the end of the limb, knowing just how far he could travel safely.

Then came the surprise. One day I glanced out to the spot where he'd been feeding, but he was no longer there. Startled, I got up and took a closer look. Piney was on the ground. My unfailing aerialist had failed. Piney had fallen.

Rushing downstairs, I ran out to him. Then I understood. The branch had snapped. It was a dead twig, and Piney lay on his back, still clinging to it with all four feet. So he hadn't failed at all, except perhaps in judgment. And that could be chalked up to inexperience.

He lay there, clutching that foot-long piece of dead wood. I hesitated to try to move him for fear he might be injured. Then he began to struggle, and I learned something more about porcupines. They are as helpless on their backs as turtles. He reached and grasped futilely, turning the stick around and around in an effort to gain support. It was only after a minute of hard exertion that he succeeded in righting himself.

No wonder the fisher-cat, the porcupine's single effective enemy in the woods, seeks to turn him over to kill him!

I also discovered something else about porcupines. Piney never again went out on that limb. Once, to test him, I got a ladder, climbed up, and set him down on the branch, but he refused to move. And I never saw him attempt a dead limb after that, either —not a small one, at least. The lesson had been learned.

This, somehow, didn't jibe with the popular notion that porkies are stupid. Of course none of us believed *that,* anyway. And to clinch the argument, Piney proceeded to learn something else. One day, purely by mistake, he backed out on the twigs farther than he had intended. The slender branch bent more and more until finally it had lowered him about three feet from the ground. He tried to claw his way back to safety, but he had gone too far. One by one the twigs and leaves gave way. Still ripping and clutching and with his tail swiveling helplessly in search of support, he dropped to the ground.

I replaced him on the big horizontal limb of the maple and thought no more of it. Five minutes later, however, when I glanced at him, he was backing out on the same little branch. And in thirty seconds more he was on the lawn again. He'd learned another lesson.

This, apparently, was fun. But it would never do. When I put him out on that tree, he was supposed to stay there. After he'd demonstrated his stunt a couple of more times, we cut off the offending limb with a saw. Again, he backed out confidently until he came to the freshly cut stub. You could almost see the surprise on his face as he swiveled his tail out in space.

We waited to see what he'd do next. He tried swinging down on several other limbs while we held our breath, but fortunately none of them drooped low enough. Apparently he was able to sense that the ground was too far away.

Of course, to get down from the tree, he could have merely descended the trunk, but its broad expanse required him to move in a spread-eagle fashion that was not very comfortable. So, barring dead twigs or going out on a limb too far, we had him where we wanted him. Putting him up in his tree was like putting him in a cage—and an edible cage at that.

"Just the same," Peg told me as we watched our small acrobat slowly make the rounds of his eighty-foot prison, "we might lose him some day. We'd better make sure we learn everything about him now."

So we put our notebook back in use. Every time he lost a quill we carefully saved it. We took photographs daily. And we tried to get his footprints.

"Tried" is just the word. It ought to be easy, we figured; just hold each foot down on a stamp pad and then press it on a piece of white paper. That's what we thought, but we hadn't consulted Piney.

Our third party wasn't exactly unwilling; I'll say that much. While Peg held him around his middle, I pressed his feet on the stamp pad. He didn't seem to mind; he just grunted a few times. But when I tried to transfer his footprint to paper, another facet of the porcupine's personality came to light. It seems that, when a porky's foot comes in contact with anything, a powerful grasping reflex is set up—unless, perhaps, he's walking on his own power. As a result, we got many smeared impressions of cupped feet, but not one that showed four toes front and five rear. We got plenty of our own fingerprints, however—plus a few palmprints, forearms, and even an elbow or two.

On the second try we decided to press his feet on the stamp pad and let him walk by himself. Having papered half the floor of the kitchen with great sheets of blank newsprint, Peg and I took off our shoes and socks so we'd make no prints of our own. And after inking Piney up, we scampered away.

The tracks were better, but by the time we'd got the last paw inked, he'd smeared the first one so that it was pretty faint. Besides, he ran directly after us, so all we got was a single line of tracks plus a few smudges on the linoleum beyond the paper.

On the third try, we got a washcloth and soaked it with ordinary writing ink. With it, we slathered up his feet. Then we dashed away as if we'd lit a firecracker on a short fuse. Slowly, we turned around to see what Piney had done.

He hadn't done a thing. The ink must have smelled good and so he merely sat down and began to lick his feet.

With the fourth try we used India ink. This did it. Apparently it wasn't as tasty. To make sure he'd create a good set of tracks, Peg and I scattered in two different directions. When he began to run toward one of us, the other called. This caused him to turn and start the other way. We did this until we had a sufficient number of prints.

It had taken only an hour, actually. Roger had offered encouragement from the sidelines, and had even got the flash camera and taken a few pictures. Then, to let Alison in on it all, he thoughtfully sent her a footprint to hang in her dorm at college.

Piney, of course, never lost his aplomb. When the ordeal was over, I wiped his feet and put him out on the porch. There he licked each foot into a copious lather—and proceeded to make perfect footprints all over the wooden floor.

The fingerprinting, photographing, and notetaking were completed none too soon. Winter in Vermont often comes on in a rush. Although porcupines do not hibernate, they're often sluggish during the cold season. Piney spent more and more of his time up on his platform, or in his den, which I'd covered with sleeping bags. By December there were entire days during which he would hardly move at all.

We kept fresh water out for him although we had to change it two or three times a day as it turned to ice. We put out three or four slices of whole wheat bread, too, plus his daily supply of oranges, peanuts, and Red Delicious apples. At least once in twenty-four hours he'd stir himself enough to sample the fruit and nuts and eat all the bread—leaving the crust like a small boy.

At Christmas time we had some friends in, following an evening of caroling. As is the custom in Vermont, they stomped the snow off their boots on the porch, brushed them with a broom, and brought them into the house. With all that stomping and sweeping, Piney roused himself enough to creep down from his perch and greet the guests.

We brought him into the house. Several members of the women's chorus were among the carolers, and they took the prickly fellow almost, but not quite literally, to their bosoms. Chattering and laughing, they paraded him into the living room by the fire, while Peg and I put the finishing touches on the egg nog.

Suddenly there was a shout. Then the whole place went dark. "Good heavens!" somebody cried. "He blew a fuse!"

I found a flashlight and went into the living room. It was full of carolers and the faint smell of burnt insulation. By the light of the fire they were all looking at the Christmas tree. It had apparently taken on a spirit of its own. Shaking and swaying, it scattered ornaments like walnuts falling after a frost.

Nobody had to tell me what had happened. It was perfectly plain. So I first pulled the electric plug. Then, getting a chair, I groped my way into the tree while Peg held the flashlight. Piney, of course, was having a grand time. Our tree this year was a hemlock, and Piney loved hemlock.

As fast as I could detach one foot, another would grab hold. Through it all the ornaments were popping, the tinsel was draped all over my head and shoulders, and those senseless carolers were laughing helplessly. Peg finally controlled herself enough to join me, and between the two of us we got the porcupine out of the tannenbaum.

After I'd replaced the fuse, we surveyed the scene. The tree had been broken about two feet from the top. Piney's sharp teeth had bitten through the wire of a set of Christmas lights in one nip; why he hadn't been fried I'll never know. And we were all sprinkled with tinsel and hemlock needles.

We put our porcupine back on the porch so the house would be safe. We straightened the tree and repaired the wire. Then we had our buffet supper. It was to have been the highlight of the evening, but after Piney's performance, it was almost an anticlimax.

Winter in Vermont is characterized by cold, deep snow, and heavy ice. One day last week a piece of ice lodged on the threshold of the door leading to the porch, and it failed to close tightly when one of us went through. Although Piney never forced his way into a tight spot—perhaps so he'd be able to back out again without dulling his quills—the door was open wide enough for his seven-pound body. Out he went into the yard, up the driveway past his climbing tree, and on to the barn.

We discovered his tracks out in the yard. Little snowy footprints went across the barn floor. Then they faded. We searched until we found him—high up under the roof of the empty hayloft. He'd climbed up the monorail of the old forklift and followed it to its highest point in the peak. There he huddled, apparently deep in his own thoughts. We called and whistled and even threw little snowballs to wake him, but to no avail. The longest ladder on the place was about eight feet too short, so we couldn't reach him, either.

This would never do. What if he came down and wandered off in the deep snow? We renewed our efforts to get him, but we couldn't penetrate his reverie.

While I fretted, Peg and Roger put apples and whole wheat bread and peanuts where he'd find them if he came down. As an afterthought, they added the teddy bear. Perhaps the food and the familiar toy would tempt him.

All of this happened just a few days ago. It's nearly maple sugaring season now. There could be a thaw any day. Possibly this will stir Piney's pudgy body to action. Then his small stomach may feel the pinch of hunger and he may climb down for a meal. And I'll be waiting for him, the little scalawag.

Then, too, this could be the long-awaited "break" with civilization which we've learned to expect from all our wild animals. He may disdain the goodies scattered over the floor and make his way up to the woods where it all started last year. Maybe he'll even get as far as Fletcher Brown's plastic pipe, festooned from one sugar maple to the next.

Perhaps that is what's about to happen. Roger

just came in from the barn. Piney has cleaned up every apple and fig bar and peanut and his tracks now lead under the foundation of the stable. The only thing left in that hayloft is the teddy bear.

If Fletcher *does* receive company, and we manage to get our hands on the quill-critter again, there's one thing Piney is going to get for sure: a spanking. He's had it coming for a long time.

I owe it to him for the geraniums, the tropical fish, the Christmas tree, the umbrella handle, and Rebel's punctured nose. I owe it to him, too, for running away like this and causing all this worry.

And just how do you spank a porcupine, anyway?

You do it gently, very gently. That's how.

With Piney there could be no other way.